# Detroit Studies in
# Music Bibliography

General Editor
**Bruno Nettl**
University of Illinois at Urbana-Champaign

# General Bibliography for Music Research

**Second Edition**

by Keith E. Mixter, *Eugene* 1922-

027231

Detroit Studies in
Music Bibliography *33*

Information Coordinators
Detroit *1975*

Cover design by Vincent Kibildis
modifies the title page of
Eucharius Zinckeisen's *Kirchen Gesang,*
a collection of Protestant church songs,
Frankfurt, 1584.

Copyright 1975 by Keith E. Mixter
Second printing 1976
Third printing 1977
Printed and bound in the United States of America
Library of Congress Catalog Card Number 72-174731
International Standard Book Number 0-911772-75-8

Published by
Information Coordinators, Inc.
1435-37 Randolph Street
Detroit, Michigan 48226

*To My Wife*

# CONTENTS

# PREFACE

I AM GRATIFIED by the reception accorded the first edition of this manual. The delay in completing the second edition is due in large part to the vastly augmented nature of the revision, although this is by no means an exhaustive bibliography, but rather a compilation of those titles deemed most useful to the music scholar.

I should like to emphasize that except for very occasional references the purpose of this handbook is to explore only non-music titles. For reference books in music the reader is referred to bibliographic aids such as Vincent Duckles' *Music Reference and Research Materials; An Annotated Bibliography* (3rd ed.; New York: The Free Press, c1974).

I am indebted to the Reference Library Staff of The Ohio State University for many helpful suggestions. My special thanks go to Professors Ruth Erlandson and Eleanor Devlin. Material for Chapter X was reviewed or expanded by the late Professor Francis L. Utley and by Professors Ana M. R. Llorens, Hans E. Keller, Albert N. Mancini, Carl C. Schlam, and Harry Vredeveld, all of The Ohio State University. I am indebted to these scholars for having given so generously of their special competencies. Finally, I am grateful to my son Christian for having read the manuscript and for having suggested improvements in so many ways.

K. E. M.

Columbus, Ohio
July 1974

# PREFACE TO FIRST EDITION

THIS STUDY is intended as a guide to the music student and music historian. I hope that it will reveal resources of bibliography that might otherwise have remained closed.

I am indebted to the Reference Library Staffs of the University of North Carolina and The Ohio State University for many helpful suggestions. My special thanks go to Miss Ruth Erlandson, Reference Librarian at the latter University, for having read the manuscript and for having offered valuable criticism and additions.

Part I of the *Syllabus for Bibliography I* of the Department of Music, University of Chicago (Syllabus Division, University of Chicago Press, 1953), now unavailable, has been a source of counsel as to order and content.

K. E. M.

# INTRODUCTION

THE PURPOSE of this study is to present in an organized manner references to general bibliographical tools that may be of aid to those engaged in research in music. In many instances, students and teachers are served by a departmental library for music; in this case acquaintance with music materials is more easily arrived at, while the realm of general library and reference materials is more remote. Even where general library and music library holdings are physically in association, a gulf often exists between the musician and non-musical reference works. This volume seeks to bridge that gulf.

Because of their general availability, few citations are made to music reference titles. In a few instances cognate works in music are cited, but only if they are directly analogous to a general work under discussion.

The emphasis herein is on titles from North America and Europe. Coverage includes books, but is not extended to articles. My concerns in description were twofold: 1) what the work in question would reveal of direct interest to the music scholar or 2) what the work might disclose of a related nature, for example in history, in the sister arts, or in the social sciences. Because of the limitations imposed on this volume the reader is encouraged to turn to comprehensive guides such as Winchell's *Guide to Reference Books* or Walford's *Guide to Reference Material* (cf. Chapter I) where further help is needed. Where limitations are particularly critical, bibliographical aids to further sources have been indicated, especially in Chapters I, II, and X.

For the purposes of this study, the terms "music" and "music literature" have been adopted to mean music to be performed and literature about music, respectively. As a matter of course, general reference works afford a much better coverage of the latter type of publication than of the former.

Since most of the works delineated in the following pages are of basic bibliographical importance, they have often been reprinted. With very few exceptions only the original printing of the latest edition is reported. Where available, full imprint information has been supplied. It is my hope that this will be of value in itself, for these facts are often difficult to procure except in bibliographical handbooks, although they are generally required in academic papers, theses, and dissertations. A dash following the date within the imprint information indicates that the work in question is still being published according to the latest information. The number of volumes is arrived at by bibliographical count, not by physical count. When not otherwise made apparent, for example by the title, the chronological scope of the work is indicated by dates enclosed in brackets. Subtitles are provided only where it is felt they would help define the nature of the publication.

# CHAPTER I / Basic Guides to Research

THE FOLLOWING TITLES, although varied in nature, are for the most part bibliographical in content. Some, while being quite old, remain indispensable tools of the field.

Before embarking on more specialized materials it might be well to mention two general guides to research. As indicated by the title, Cecil B. Williams and Allan H. Stevenson's *A Research Manual for College Studies and Papers* (rev. ed.; New York: Harper, 1951) is directed toward college and university work. Primarily a manual for historians, Jacques Barzun and Henry F. Graff's *The Modern Researcher* (rev. ed.; New York: Harcourt, [1970]) is written in a lively manner and contains some discussion of problems of music research.[1]

## Style Manuals

A guide to general English practice is H. W. Fowler's *A Dictionary of Modern English Usage* (2nd ed.; Oxford: The Clarendon Press, 1965). This edition, revised by Sir Ernest Gowers, is greatly enhanced by the addition of a classified guide. In problems of style, the Chicago University Press *A Manual of Style* (12th ed.; Chicago: University of Chicago Press, 1969) is the accepted guide for many scholarly journals. If the work in progress is not destined for publication, but will remain in typescript, Kate L. Turabian's *A Manual for Writers of Term Papers, Theses, and Dissertations* (4th ed.; Chicago: University of Chicago Press, [1973]) is very valuable and is recommended by many graduate schools. A smaller volume, containing valuable suggestions for style in writing English, is *The Elements of Style* (New York: Macmillan, [1959]) by William Strunk and E. B. White.[2]

---

[1] Ruth T. Watanabe, in part 2 of her *Introduction to Music Research* (Englewood Cliffs: Prentice-Hall, 1967), discusses various facets of the selection and organization of a research paper, including matters of style.

[2] We should like to point to two style manuals written expressly for the music scholar. These are Demar Irvine's *Writing About Music; A Style Book for Reports and Theses* (Seattle: University of Washington Press, c1968), whose revised edition contains new material intended to provide suggestions for the improvement of literary style, and Eugene Helm and Albert T. Luper, *Words and Music* (Hackensack, N.J.: Boonin, c1971).

Problems arising from dealing with foreign languages may be solved by use of the U.S. Government Printing Office *Style Manual* (rev. ed.; Washington: U.S. Government Printing Office, 1967), which lists common abbreviations used in each language. Georg F. von Ostermann's *Manual of Foreign Languages for the Use of Librarians, Bibliographers, Research Workers, Editors, Translators, and Printers* (4th ed.; New York: Central Book Co., 1952) discusses the treatment of each language and covers such items as alphabets, diacritical marks, languages and monies of the world, and library and bibliographical terms.

A guide to the procedure of indexing is provided in Robert L. Collison's *Indexes and Indexing* (3rd rev. ed.; London: Benn, 1969). The volume contains a chapter on "The Indexing of Music and Recordings." A. C. Foskett's *A Guide to Personal Indexes* ([Hamdon, Conn.] : Archon, 1967) suggests ways to arrange personal indexes so that they may be made adaptable to a mechanical retrieval system. Finally, mention should be made of *A Guide to Book Publishing* by Datus C. Smith (New York: Bowker, c1966), a volume which discusses the relationship of authors to the book trade.

## Reference Works

In the area of reference works, the older manual by Isadore G. Mudge, *Guide to Reference Books* (6th ed.; Chicago: American Library Association, 1936) is superseded by Constance M. Winchell's publication of the same name (8th ed.; Chicago: American Library Association, 1967). Supplements to the excellent Winchell volume have appeared both as book publications and as articles in the January and July issues of *College and Research Libraries* (since January 1952).

Other publications in this field are John Minto, *Reference Books* (London: The Library Association, 1929), Louis Shores, *Basic Reference Sources* (Chicago: American Library Association, 1954), and Albert J. Walford, *Guide to Reference Material* (3 vols., 2nd ed.; [London] : The Library Association, 1966–70). Volume 3 of this well-annotated work covers the arts. In Rolland E. Stevens' *Reference Books in the Social Sciences and Humanities* (3rd ed., Champaign, Ill.: Illini Union Bookstore, 1971) one finds, among others, sections devoted to Music, Fine Arts, and Theatre and Dance.

## Bibliographic Guides

Treatises on bibliography in general are Henry B. Van Hoesen, *Bibliography, Practical, Enumerative, Historical* (New York and London: Scribner and Sons, 1928), Georg Schneider, *Theory and History of Bibliography*, translated by Ralph Shaw (New York: Scarecrow, 1962), and Arundell Esdaile, *A Manual of Bibliography* (4th ed.; London: Allen & Unwin and The Library Association, [1967]). Two volumes which are directed toward the description of older literature such as incunabula are Fredson Bowers, *Principles of Bibliographical Description* (Princeton: Princeton University Press, 1949) and Roland B. McKerrow, *An Introduction to Bibliography for Literary Students* (Oxford: Clarendon Press, 1927), the latter covering the mechanics of early book production.[3]

French and German publications are Louise N. Malclès, *Les Sources du travail bibliographique* (3 vols.; Genève: E. Droz, 1950-58) and Fritz Milkau, *Handbuch der Bibliothekswissenschaft* (2. Auflage; Wiesbaden: Harrassowitz, 1950-). The latter, as is indicated by the title, embraces much more than bibliography.

## Works on History

Music historians will find Ernst Bernheim's *Lehrbuch der historischen Methode und der Geschichtsphilosophie* (5th and 6th ed.; Leipzig: Duncker & Humblot, 1914) to be the classical work in the area of general historiography, while J. H. J. Van der Pot, *De Periodisering der Geschiedenis; Een Overzicht der Theorieën* ('s-Gravenhage: W. P. van Stockum en Zoon, 1951) discusses the theories of periodization which have prevailed in historiography. Helen J. Poulton presents a chapter on "Guides, Manuals, and Bibliographies of History" in her *The Historian's Handbook* (Norman: University of Oklahoma Press, 1972).

The American Historical Association's *Guide to Historical Literature* (New York: Macmillan, 1961) lists the aids and literature for the study of the history of the individual countries. Over eighty titles may be found classified under "Music" in the Library of Congress' *Guide to the Study of the United States of America* (Washington: Library of Congress, 1960). In geographical matters, the *Historical Atlas* by William R. Shepherd (9th ed.; New York: Barnes & Noble, 1964) can be consulted. A key to older place names is provided through Christine Blackie's *A Dictionary of Place-Names, Giving Their Derivations* (3rd ed.; London: Murray, 1887) or Johann G. T. Grässe's *Orbis latinus; Oder, Verzeichnis der wichtigsten lateinischen Orts- und Ländernamen* (3. Auflage; Berlin: Schmidt, 1922), while special emphasis on religious institutions may be found in L. H. Gottineau's *Répertoire topo-bibliographique des abbayes et prieures* (2 vols.; Mâcon: Protat, 1939).

---

[3] The application of the technique of book description to a musical problem may be seen in Glen Haydon, "The First Edition of Kerle's Hymns: 1558 or 1560?" *Acta Musicologica* XXXVIII (1966), 179-84.

## Treatises on Dating and Paleography

Recent research has demonstrated the usefulness of watermarks in the dating of manuscript music.[4] Two general works on watermarks are Charles M. Briquet, *Les filigranes; Dictionnaire historique des marques du papier* (4 vols., 2nd ed.; Leipzig: Hiersemann, 1923) and the more recent volume by Edward Heawood, *Watermarks, Mainly of the 17th and 18th Centuries* (Hilversum: Paper Publications Society, 1950).

In problems of chronology, John J. Bond's *Handy-Book of Rules and Tables for Verifying Dates with the Christian Era* (4th ed.; London: Bell, 1889) and Hermann Grotefend's *Zeitrechnung des deutschen Mittelalters und der Neuzeit* (2 vols.; Hannover: Hahn, 1891–98) are valuable. The latter is particularly helpful in the matter of liturgical calendars. A condensation of this book is Grotefend's *Taschenbuch der Zeitrechnung des deutschen Mittelalters und der Neuzeit* (Hannover: Hahnsche Buchhandlung, 1960), which has gone through a tenth edition benefited by contributions from the Lower-Rhine and Flemish areas. The *Manuel de diplomatique* by Arthur Giry (Paris: Hachette, 1894) not only treats of chronology and dating, but also contains information on medieval documents.

R. B. Hasleden's *Scientific Aids for the Study of Manuscripts* ([London]: Oxford University Press, 1935) discusses the application of scientific procedures such as light filters and the ultraviolet lamp to an examination of the script and physical structure of the manuscript. Two handbooks of paleography are those by Maurice Prou, *Manuel de paléographie latine et française* (4. éd.; Paris: Picard, 1924) and Berthold Louis Ullman, *Ancient Writing and Its Influence* (New York: Longmans, 1932). The latter contains particularly valuable information on regional hands of the Middle Ages. For the student of paleography and the history of musical notation, the *Lexicon abbreviaturarum; Dizionario di abbreviature latine ed italiane,* by Adriano Cappelli (6. ed.; Milano: Hoepli, 1961), is an indispensable tool in the deciphering of abbreviations and similar signs. A supplement to this manual is Auguste Pelzer's *Abréviations latines médiévales* (2e ed.; Paris: Beatrice-Nauwelaerts, 1966).

---

4 See especially Jan Larué, "Watermarks and Musicology," *Acta Musicologica* XXIII (1961), 120-46, with an extended bibliography.

# CHAPTER II / Bibliographies of Bibliographies

ALTHOUGH MANY BIBLIOGRAPHIES contain sections devoted to a listing of bibliographies, this chapter will, with few exceptions, present only those works which are entirely registers of bibliographies.

Such publications may be divided into two general categories. The first of these includes those titles which are of a general nature, and the second embraces those which are specialized in their viewpoints, usually according to subject matter.

## General Bibliographies

Theodore Besterman's *A World Bibliography of Bibliographies* (5 vols., 4th ed.; Lausanne: Societas Bibliographica, 1965–66) is extremely comprehensive. Included therein are references to one hundred seventeen thousand items, under sixteen thousand headings and sub-headings. The coverage has been brought down to 1963, inclusive, and the text has been minutely revised. Of particular interest to the musical scholar are the listings of library catalogues and the entries for individual composers. Under the latter, indexes to works and similar items may be found. Seventy-two columns are devoted to music. The fifth volume of the set, the index volume, lists, among other things, authors, editors, translators, titles, libraries, and archives. Robert L. Collison's *Bibliographies, Subject and National; A Guide to Their Contents, Arrangement, and Use* (3rd ed.; London: Lockwood, 1968) is divided into two large parts, "Subject Bibliographies" and "Universal and National Bibliographies." A recent publication outlining bibliographies which appear in serial form is Richard A. Gray's *Serial Bibliographies in the Humanities and Social Sciences* (Ann Arbor: Pieran, 1969). Over thirty items are in the area of music.

Two post-war German bibliographies are Wilhelm Totok, Rolf Weitzel and Karl-Heinz Weimann, *Handbuch der bibliographischen Nachschlagewerke* (3rd ed.; Frankfurt am Main: Klostermann, [1966]) and the *Internationale Bibliographie der Bibliographien* by Hanns Bohatta and Franz Hodes (Frankfurt am Main: Kostermann, [1950]). In the former, "Musikwissenschaft,"

occupying nearly four pages, is found under "Künste" in the section on
"Fachbibliographien," while in the latter music is entered under "Kunstwis-
senschaft" and extends to fifteen columns. Typical divisions in the Bohatta
and Hodes work are "Allgemeines," "Instrumentalmusik," and "Opern."
John Minto's *Reference Books* (cf. Chapter I), although having a relatively
small section on music (seven columns), demonstrates a useful emphasis on
local English history. Of the older German bibliographies Julius Petzholdt's
*Bibliotheca bibliographica; Kritisches Verzeichnis der das Gesamtgebiet der
Bibliographie betreffendenden Literatur des In- und Auslandes in systematischer
Ordnung* (Leipzig: Engelmann, 1886) is still to be recommended because of its
critical annotations, as is the fourth German edition of Georg Schneider's
*Handbuch der Bibliographie* (Leipzig: Hiersemann, 1930) because of its
incunabula indexes and bibliographies of society publications. Winchell's
*Guide to Reference Books* (cf. Chapter I) contains a section on "Bibliography,"
under which may be found general works, lists of library catalogues, national
and trade bibliographies, and volumes on printing and publishing, book
illustration, and bookbinding.

Older treatises, which may therefore enter useful titles that have since
become obscure, are William P. Courtney, *A Register of National Bibliography*
(3 vols.; London: Constable, 1905-12), Henry Stein, *Manuel de bibliographie
générale* (Paris: Picard, 1897), and Léon Vallée *Bibliographie des bibliographies*
(2 vols.; Paris: Terquem, 1883-87).

*The Bibliographic Index; A Cumulative Bibliography of Bibliographies*
[1937-] (New York: Wilson, 1938-) is issued in serial form. The first
cumulation (published in 1945, covering the years 1937-42) has eighteen
columns devoted to music, with subject headings following the Library of
Congress system. Cumulations for the following years devote from four to
six columns to music. Beginning with the 1951-55 cumulation the subject
headings include "Musicology." Much literature not essentially bibliographical
can be found here, since such pieces are listed for the bibliographies to be
found within them. Prior to about 1949 (the date of the inception of the
*Music Index*[1]), music periodicals indexed were *Music and Letters*, *Music Clubs
Magazine*, *Music Educators Journal*, *Musical Quarterly*, *Music Review*, and
*Music Library Association Notes*, but the music specialist should bear in mind
that such bibliographies as *The Bibliographic Index* serve as invaluable guides
to music literature in non-music journals.

Two German publications are issued in serial form. The *Bibliographische
Berichte*, edited by Erich Zimmermann and sponsored by the Deutsches
Bibliographisches Kuratorium (Frankfurt am Main: Klostermann, 1959),
appears quarterly. The arrangement is by subject, with an annual index, and

---

[1] Detroit: Information Coordinators, Inc., 1949-.

the coverage is international in scope. The *Bibliographie der deutschen Bibliographien* (12 vols.; Leipzig: Verlag für Buch- und Bibliothekswesen, 1954–65) is continued in the *Bibliographie der deutschen Bibliographien; Monatliches Verzeichnis* (Leipzig: Verlag für Buch- und Bibliothekswesen, 1966–), which provides also a yearly index. Music is covered in section 11, "Musik, Tanz, Theater, Film, Rundfunk, Fernsehen."

The *Index Bibliographicus; Directory of Current Periodical Abstracts and Bibliographies* (4th ed.; La Haye: Fédération Internationale de Documentation, 1959–) will include humanities within its volume 3. The organization is by Universal Decimal Classification, and the business addresses of periodicals are given. Paul Ancienne's *Bibliographical Services Throughout the World, 1960–1964* ([Paris] : UNESCO, [1969]) discusses current bibliographies of special subjects, among other topics.

## Specialized Bibliographies

Among the specialized bibliographies of bibliographies are two which are devoted to history. The first of these is Edith M. Coulter and Melanie Gerstenfeld, *Historical Bibliographies; A Systematic and Annotated Guide* (Berkeley: University of California Press, 1935). The work is organized first by general bibliographies and then in a chronological or geographical manner. American history is represented by Henry Putney Beers' *Bibliographies in American History; Guide to Materials for Research* (2nd ed.; New York: Wilson, 1942). Music is accorded forty-four titles, and these are amplified by further references in the index.

General catalogues of manuscripts can be found listed in Clark S. Northrup, *Register of Bibliographies of the English Language and Literature* (New Haven: Yale University Press, 1925). Theodore Besterman's *Early Printed Books to the End of the Sixteenth Century; A Bibliography of Bibliographies* (2nd ed.; Genève: Societas Bibliographica, 1961) provides twenty-four items on music. There are large subdivisions according to block books and books printed from type, with five indexes. A unique work for the specialist in American music is Lawrence B. Romaine's *A Guide to American Trade Catalogs, 1744–1900* (New York: Bowker, 1960).[2] Catalogues of musical instruments and accessories are entered, together with the locations of copies.

Helen F. Conover's *Current National Bibliographies* (Washington: Library of Congress, 1955) lists bibliographies by country. While there is no subject index,

---

[2] The interested reader is referred to this same author's "Pictorial Records of Musical Instruments in 19th-Century American Trade Catalogs," *Music Library Association Notes* XVIII (1960–61), 383–96.

these sections do include separate music bibliographies, where they exist, or discuss parts of larger publications which deal with music. Five columns are devoted to music in Arthur Gropp's *A Bibliography of Latin American Bibliographies* (Metuchen, N.J.: Scarecrow, 1968). John G. Barrows' annotated *Bibliography of Bibliographies in Religion* (Ann Arbor: Edwards, 1955) covers the literature to 1950 and gives locations. A separate chapter for music (Chapter 10) is provided in Richard H. Rouse's *Serial Bibliographies for Medieval Studies* (Berkeley: University of California Press, [1969]), with further cross references.

Over four thousand annotated summaries and bibliographies are provided under author and subject in *Bibliographies and Summaries in Education to July 1935* (New York: Wilson, 1936), by Walter S. Monroe and Louis Shores. For subsequent literature one should refer to the *Education Index* (cf. Chapter VIII). Films, filmstrips, kinescopes, phonodiscs, phonotapes, programed instruction materials, slides, transparencies, and videotapes are listed in *Guides to New Educational Media* (2nd ed.; Chicago: American Library Association, 1967), by Margaret I. Rufsvold and Carolyn Guss. The index reflects "Music."

# CHAPTER III / National and Trade Bibliographies

A NATIONAL BIBLIOGRAPHY is a list of books produced in one country. It may include books about the country by natives of that country regardless of residence as well as books produced in that country without regard to language. It is usually an official publication of the government of that nation. A trade bibliography, on the other hand, is a catalogue of books in print and available at any given time in a given area, with emphasis on book promotion and sale.

The publications of William P. Courtney and Helen F. Conover (cf. Chapter II) are bibliographical guides to these types of works. In addition, an account of early national bibliography is given in LeRoy H. Linder, *The Rise of Current Complete National Bibliography* (New York: Scarecrow, 1959), in which several music bibliographies are discussed. Knud Larsen, in his *National Bibliographical Services, Their Creation and Operation* (Paris: UNESCO, 1953), provides for the novice a detailed and very useful explanation of the rationale of bibliography, particularly in reference to national bibliography.

For the purposes of this study a bibliography still in progress is considered current; one which has ceased publication is treated as retrospective. Some bibliographies classed as "current" have such long publishing histories that they are also of value historically. By observing the dates of publication it will be apparent which titles may be so considered. In the following listings, where the period of coverage is not evident from the title or from the imprint, it is shown in brackets appended to the title.

National and trade bibliographies may be of importance to the historian in two distinct ways. The current bibliographies disclose information concerning the existence and availability of material in his field, while retrospective bibliographies are a record of titles which have been published in the past. In the following account the concentration for foreign countries will be on national bibliography, rather than on trade bibliographies, for the coverage of music in the former is somewhat better than in the latter.

## Current Bibliographies

Of special interest to the musician is an informative article by Donald W. Krummel and James B. Coover which outlines the uses of current national bibliographies for the field of music.[1] Many national bibliographies make use of the Universal Decimal Classification, in which music is found under the number "78."

THE UNITED STATES—In the United States, bibliographies are the *Publisher's Weekly* (New York: [various publishers], 1872-), of which the *American Book Publishing Record* (New York: Bowker, 1960-), with its annual index, is a monthly cumulation; the *Publisher's Trade List Annual* (New York: [various publishers], 1873-), of which *Books in Print* (New York: Bowker, 1948-) is the author-title-series index and *Subject Guide to Books in Print* (New York: Bowker, 1957-) is the subject index; and the *Cumulative Book Index* (Minneapolis and New York: Wilson, 1898-). The last is issued on a monthly basis and is cumulated. Ralph N. Schoolcraft's *Performing Arts / Books in Print; An Annotated Bibliography* (New York: Drama Book Specialists, 1973) contains rather lengthy sections on the "musical theatre." Because of the meteoric rise of paperback book publication in recent years, one should note *Paperbound Books in Print* (New York: Bowker, 1955-). The above are, of course, valuable for their book listings. A valuable key to microform publications are the *Guide to Microforms in Print* (Washington: Microcard Editions, 1961-) and its *Subject Guide to Microforms in Print* [1962/63-] (Washington: Microcard Editions, 1962-). Music is served under the number "790." The best consultant for music is the U.S. Copyright Office, *Catalog of Copyright Entries* (Washington: Government Printing Office, 1891-). Winchell's *Guide* gives the history and application of the set. Music, both American and foreign, which has been deposited in the Copyright Office, has been recorded here since 1906, when the new series began. In the period 1906-45 published and unpublished music was entered monthly in one alphabetical series, followed by renewals. An annual index was provided. In 1946 entries fell into three groups: unpublished music, published music, and renewals. A title index to the first two groups was included. From 1947 to 1956 the catalogue appeared semiannually, with music as part 5 A (all published music, arranged alphabetically, with cross references and a title index; beginning with the second half of 1948 there has been a title index), part 5 B (unpublished music, by title), and part 14 B or 5 C (renewals, by title). From 1957 on these parts have been unified and called part 5, which has an index referring to composers, text writers, editors, compilers, arrangers, and

---

1 "Current National Bibliographies; Their Music Coverage," *Music Library Association Notes* XVII (1959-60), 375-88.

claimants. In view of the significant writings on music occasionally issued as government publications, the bibliographical control offered by the U.S. Superintendent of Documents' *Monthly Catalog of the United States Government Publications* (Washington: Government Printing Office, 1895-) is of considerable importance. The *Vertical File Index* [1932-] (New York: Wilson, 1935-) gives valuable information about pamphlets and similar material through a title and subject index.

BRITAIN AND THE BRITISH COMMONWEALTH—For Great Britain an excellent source is the *British National Bibliography* (London: Council of the British National Bibliography, 1950-), which covers music literature, with indexes by author, title, and subject, cumulated every five years.[2] Use may also be made of *Whitaker's Cumulative Book List* (London: Whitaker, 1924-), for the entire United Kingdom, and the *English Catalogue of Books* [1801-] (London: [various publishers], 1864-). Mention should also be made of *British Books in Print; The Reference Catalogue of Current Literature* (London: Whitaker, 1965-) and *Paperbacks in Print* (London: Whitaker, 1960-), the latter being issued on a semiannual basis.

Acquisitions in music and music literature by the National Library in Ottawa are listed in *Canadiana* (Ottawa: National Library of Canada, 1951-). The *Australian National Bibliography* (Canberra: National Library of Australia, 1961-) lists music literature.

WESTERN EUROPE—The *Bibliographie de la France* (Paris: [various publishers], 1811-) appears weekly and contains books. Music (covered since 1811!) is now contained in Supplement C of the "Bibliographie officielle," while theses are found in Supplement D. "Les livres de l'année" is the annual cumulation of part 3 of the *Bibliographie*. It contains a classified index. French books in print are covered in the *Catalogue des livres disponibles* (Paris: Cercle de la Librairie, 1969-).

The *Deutsche National-Bibliographie* (Leipzig: [various publishers], 1931-) is issued in three series. Reihe A represents "Neuerscheinungen des Buchhandels," appearing weekly, with a quarter-annual "Verfasser- u. Stichwortregister." Reihe B contains "Neuerscheinungen ausserhalb des Buchhandels" and appears semimonthly, with quarter-annual indexes. Reihe C, published since 1968, lists "Dissertationen und Habilitations-schriften." The *Jahresverzeichnis des deutschen Schrifttums* [1945/46-] (Leipzig: Verlag des Börsenvereins der deutschen Buchhändler, 1948-) is an annual cumulation of both series. The *Deutsches Bücherverzeichnis* [1911-] (Leipzig: [various publishers], 1915-) presents five-year cumulations.

---

[2] Music itself is covered in the *British Catalogue of Music* (London: Council of the British National Bibliography, 1957-). ,

WESTERN EUROPE *(Continued)*—West Germany is represented in two lists
issued by the Deutsche Bibliothek in Frankfurt, the weekly *Deutsche
Bibliographie* (Frankfurt am Main: [various publishers], 1947-) and the
*Deutsche Bibliographie; Halbjahresverzeichnis* (Frankfurt am Main:
Büchhandler-Vereinigung, 1951-), the latter being a semiannual cumulation
of the former, which, since 1965, is appearing in three series (A, publications
in the book trade; B, publications not in the book trade; and C, maps).
Quinquennial cumulations are published under the title *Deutsche
Bibliographie; Fünfjahresverzeichnis* [1945/50] (Frankfurt am Main:
Buchhändler-Vereinigung, 1953-).[3]
     In Austria the *Österreichische Bibliographie* (Wien: [various publishers],
1946-) has covered music itself since 1958 in a "Sonderheft." Those
searching for Swiss music and music literature should consult *Das Schweizer
Buch / Le Livre suisse / Il libro svizzero* (Bern-Bümpliz: Benteli, 1901-),
with quinquennial cumulations in the *Schweizer Bücherverzeichnis /
Répertoire du livre suisse / Elenco del libro svizzero* [1948/50-] (Zürich:
Schweizerischer Buchhandler- und Verlegerverein, 1951-).
     The *Bibliographie de Belgique* (Bruxelles: Bibliothèque Royale, 1875-)
appears monthly, and music and books on music can be found here. Books
and music, as well as important periodical articles, are listed in the
*Bibliographie luxembourgeoise* [1944/45-] (Luxembourg: Bibliothèque
Nationale, 1946-). For the Netherlands, *Brinkman's cumulatieve catalogus
van boeken* (Leiden: Sijthoff, 1846-) classifies music and books on music,
as does the index volume of *Brinkman's catalogus van boeken, plaat- en
kaartwerken* [1850-] (Amsterdam/Leiden: [various publishers], 1883-).
The latter is published in five-year cumulations.
     In Denmark's *Dansk Bogfortegnelse* [1841/58-] (København: Gads,
1861-) music books and music are covered. The yearly issues are entitled
*Årskatalog* (København: Gads, 1851-). Norway is represented by the
*Norsk bogfortegnelse* [1814/47-] ([place varies: various publishers], 1848-),
which also issues an annual *Årskatalog* [1952-] (Oslo: Norske Bokhandler-
forening, 1953-). Music is generally found under "Kunst." Sweden possesses
separate music bibliographies,[4] but music books and song books are to be
found in the *Svensk bokförteckning* (Stockholm: Tidningsaktiebolaget
Svensk Bokhandel, 1953-). Finland's book production is subject to
bibliographical control in the *Suomessa ilmestyneen kirjallisuuden luettelo;*

---

3 For German music coverage the reader is directed to the *Hofmeisters Handbuch der
Musikliteratur* (Leipzig: Hofmeister, 1844-) or the *Jahresverzeichnis der deutschen
Musikalien und Musikschriften* (Leipzig: Hofmeister, 1852-).
     4 Cf. Krummel and Coover, *op. cit.*, 383. Separate music bibliographies for other
countries, where existing, are also listed in this article.

*Katalog över i Finland utkommen Litteratur* [1945-] (Helsinki: Suomalaisen Kirjallisuuden Seuran Kirjapainon Oy, [1950-]), which appears quarterly.

In Spain, the monthly *Boletín del depósito legal de obras impresas* (Madrid: Dirección General de Archivos y Bibliotecas, 1958-) provides monthly coverage of music, music literature, and phonograph records, while the *Bibliografía española* [1958-] (Madrid: Ministerio de Educacíon Nacional, 1959-) presents an annual listing of music and music literature. Music and music literature is covered in the *Boletim de bibliografia portuguesa* [1935-] (Lisboa: Biblioteca Nacional, 1937-). The *Bollettino* of the Italian Ufficio della Proprietà Letteraria, Artistica e Scientifica (Roma, Ufficio della Proprietà Letteraria, Artistica e Scientifica, 1945-) provides a monthly listing of Italian music and phonograph records, while a monthly coverage of music literature may be found in the *Bibliografia nazionale italiana* (Firenze: Biblioteca Nazionale Centrale, 1958-), with music being represented in an annual supplement entitled "Testi Musicali."

EASTERN EUROPE—Yugoslavian and Greek production may be found in the *Bibliografija jugoslavije* (Beograd: Bibliografski Institut FNRJ, 1950-) and the *Bulletin analytique de bibliographie hellénique* (Athènes: Institut Français d'Athènes, 1947-), respectively. Music of Czech and Slovak origin can be located in the weekly *Bibliografický katalog Československé Republiky* (V Praze: Nákladem Ministerstva Školství a Národní Osvěty, 1933-).

Hungary is represented by the *Magyar nemzeti bibliográfia* (Budapest: Országos Széchényi Könyvtár, 1946-), while the Rumanian *Anuarul cărții din Republica Populară Romînă* [1952/54-] (Bucureşti: [various publishers], 1957-), issued by the Biblioteca Centrală de Stat, includes "Note Muzicale." Bulgarian production is covered in *Bulgarski knigopis* (Sofia: Narodna Biblioteka, 1897-), while Polish music and music literature may be found in *Przewodnik bibliograficzny* (Warszawa: Biblioteka Narodowa, 1946-). National bibliographies of the USSR are brought under bibliographical control in *Gosudarstvennaia bibliografia SSSR; Spravochnik* (2nd ed.; Moskva: Kniga, 1967), but in regard to Russian music and music literature one should refer to the *Knizhnaya letopis'* (Moskva: [various publishers], 1907-), which is cumulated on a selected basis in *Ezhegodnik knigi* SSSR [1941-] (Moskva: Izd-vo Vsesoiuznoi Kniznoi Palaty, 1946-). Greater accessibility is afforded to many readers through the *Monthly Index of Russian Accessions* (Washington: Government Printing Office, 1948-), compiled by the Library of Congress and provided with a subject index. Music, music literature, and periodicals on music are listed, with titles given in translation and in transliteration.

## Retrospective Bibliographies

INTERNATIONAL COVERAGE—Two sets international in scope are Jacques Charles Brunet, *Manuel du libraire et de l'amateur de livres* (9 vols., 5. éd.; Paris: Didot, 1860-80) and Johann Grässe, *Trésor de livres rares et precieux* (7 vols.; Dresden: Kuntze, 1859-69). The British Museum has published a series of "short title catalogues" which affords retrospective coverage to ca.1600 for France, Italy, Spain, the Netherlands, and Belgium, German-speaking countries, Portugal, Spain, and Hispanic America.

Unfortunately the coverage of music itself is minimal in most of the sets discussed in this section devoted to retrospective bibliographies. For this reason the reader will want to take cognizance of the fair catalogues, especially those of Leipzig and Frankfurt (from ca.1564), which are unique early sources of music bibliography.[5]

THE UNITED STATES—In the United States the following years are covered by these retrospective bibliographies: 1639-1800, Charles Evans, *American Bibliography* (14 vols.; [place varies: various publishers], 1903-59), together with the *Supplement to Charles Evans' American Bibliography* compiled by Roger P. Bristol (Charlottesville: University of Virginia Press, [1970]);[6] 1801-19, Ralph R. Shaw and Richard H. Shoemaker, *American Bibliography; A Preliminary Checklist, 1801-1819* (22 vols.; New York and London: Scarecrow Press, 1958-66); 1820-61, Orville A. Roorbach, *Biblioteca Americana* (4 vols.; New York: Roorbach, 1852-61) and Richard H. Shoemaker, *Checklist of American Imprints, 1820-* (New York: Scarecrow, 1964-), which is planned as an improvement over Roorbach in completeness, accuracy, and the provision of locations; 1861-71, James Kelly, *American Catalogue of Books* (2 vols.; New York: Wiley, 1866-71); 1876-1910, *American Catalogue of Books* (9 vols.; New York: Publishers' Weekly, 1876-1910). A valuable adjunct to these is Joseph Sabin, *Biblioteca Americana* (29 vols.; New York: [privately printed], 1868-1936).

Confederate sheet music can be found in Marjorie L. Crandall, *Confederate Imprints* (2 vols.; Boston: Athenaeum, 1955) and in Richard B. Harwell, *More Confederate Imprints* (2 vols.; Richmond: Virginia State Library, 1957). Early music imprints from various states are listed in the *Historical Records Survey; American Imprints Inventory* (Washington: Historical Records Survey, 1937-42), the volumes and contents of which are described in Winchell's *Guide*.

---

5 See Albert Göhler, "Die Messkataloge im Dienste der musikalischen Geschichtsforschung," *Sammelbände der Internationalen Musikgesellschaft* 3 (1901-2): 294-376.

6 The specialist should note the existence of Donald L. Hixon, *Music in Early America; A Bibliography of Music in Evans* (Metuchen, N.J.: Scarecrow, 1970). Part 1, the largest, includes all items available in the *Early American Imprints* microprint edition. There is a composer-compiler index and a title index.

BRITAIN AND CANADA—British coverage is as follows: 1475-1640, A. W. Pollard and G. R. Redgrave, *A Short-Title Catalogue of Books Printed in England, Scotland, and Ireland, and of English Books Printed Abroad, 1475-1640* (London: The Bibliographical Society, 1926); and 1641-1700, Donald G. Wing, *Short-Title Catalogue of Books Printed in England, Scotland, Ireland, Wales, and British America and of English Books Printed in Other Countries, 1641-1700* (2nd ed.; New York: The Modern Language Association, 1972-). Paul Morrison has published indexes to these publications (Charlottesville: Bibliographical Society of the University of Virginia, 1950 and 1955, respectively). Sets to be used with the foregoing are Edward Arber, *A Transcript of the Registers of the Company of Stationers of London, 1554-1640 A.D.* (5 vols.; London and Birmingham: [privately printed], 1875-94), *A Transcript of the Registers of the Worshipful Company of Stationers, from 1640-1708 A.D.* (3 vols.; London: [privately printed], 1913-14), and Edward Arber, *The Term Catalogues, 1668-1709 A.D., with a Number for Easter Term 1711 A.D.* (3 vols.; London: Arber, 1903-6). The first Arber work is indexed and to some extent supplemented by Walter W. Greg, *A Companion to Arber; Being a Calendar of Documents in Edward Arber's "Transcript of the Registers of the Company of Stationers of London, 1554-1640," with Text and Calendar of Supplementary Documents* (Oxford: Clarendon, 1967). For the eighteenth and nineteenth centuries the reader is referred to the *London Catalogue of Books* (London: [various publishers], 1773 and various years following).

Limited bibliographical control for Ireland is provided through Ernest R. M. Dix's *Catalogue of Early Dublin-Printed Books, 1601-1700* (4 vols. and supplements; Dublin: [O'Donoghue], 1898-1912), which includes books, tracts, broadsides, and similar material. Canadian books published from 1759 to 1867 are listed, mainly by author, with no subject index, in Henry J. Morgan's *Bibliotheca Canadensis; Or a Manual of Canadian Literature* (Ottawa: Desbarats, 1867), while a somewhat later period of Canadian coverage is afforded in Willet R. Haight's *Canadian Catalogue of Books, 1791-1897* (3 vols.; Toronto: Haight, 1896-1904).

WESTERN EUROPE—For France, in roughly chronological order, one has Avenir Tchemerzine, *Bibliographie d'éditions originales et rares d'auteurs français des XV<sup>e</sup>, XVI<sup>e</sup>, XVII<sup>e</sup>, et XVIII<sup>e</sup> siècles* (10 vols.; Paris: Plée, 1927-34); *Répertoire bibliographique des livres imprimés en France au seizième siècle* (Baden-Baden: Heitz, 1968-); Joseph Marie Quérard, *La France littéraire . . . XVIII<sup>e</sup> et XIX<sup>e</sup> siècles* (12 vols; Paris: Didot, 1827-64); the same author's *La littérature française contemporaraine* [1827-49] (6 vols.; Paris: Daguin, 1842-57); and *Catalogue général de la librairie française* [1840-1925] (34 vols.; Paris: [various publishers], 1867-1945), by Otto Lorenz and others.

WESTERN EUROPE *(Continued)*—In Germany the following years are covered
by these respective publications.' 1700-1892, Wilhelm Heinsius, *Allgemeines
Bücher-Lexikon* (19 vols.; Leipzig: [various publishers], 1812-94);
1750-1910, Christian Gottlob Kayser, *Vollständiges Bücher-Lexikon*
(42 vols.; Leipzig: [various publishers], 1834-1912); and 1797-1944,
*Halbjahresverzeichnis der Neuerscheinungen des deutschen Buchhandels*
(292 vols.; Leipzig: Börsenverein der Deutschen Buchhändler, 1798-1944).
    Early coverage, through about the seventeenth century, for the territory
now known as Belgium, is provided in the *Bibliotheca Belgica* (in three
series; Gand / La Haye / Bruxelles: [various publishers], 1880-1964),
Jean François Foppens' *Bibliotheca Belgica* (2 vols.; Bruxelles: Foppens,
1738), and the more recent *Belgica Typographica 1541-1600* (Nieuwkoop:
DeGraaf, 1968-), by Elly Cockx-Indestege and Geneviève Glorieux, in which
composers are given attention. The *Bibliographie Nationale* (4 vols.;
Bruxelles: Weissenbruch, 1886-1910) gives production for the years 1830-80.
Flemish publications may be found in Theophiel Coopman and Jan Broeckaert,
*Bibliographie van den Vlaamschen taalstrijd* [1787-1886] (10 vols.; Gent:
Siffer, 1904-14) and in Fr. de Potter, *Vlaamsche bibliographie* (Gent: Siffer,
1893-[1902]), which covers the period 1830 to 1890 and which includes
"Muziekwerken." For the Netherlands the bibliographies are as follows:
1500-1540, Wouter Nijhoff and M. E. Kronenberg, *Nederlandsche
bibliographie* (in three parts; 's Gravenhage: Nijhoff, 1923-61); 1600-1787,
Johannes van Abkoude, *Naamregister van de . . . Nederduitsche boeken*
(2nd ed.; Rotterdam: Arrenberg, 1788); 1790-1832, the same author's
*Alphabetische naamlijst van boeken* ('s Gravenhage: van Cleef, 1835); and
1833-49, C. L. Brinkman, *Alphabetische naamlijst van boeken, plaat- en
kaartwerken* (Amsterdam: Brinkman, 1858).
    A 1961 reprint of the *Bibliotheca Danica* [1482-1830] (4 vols.;
København: Gyldendal, 1877-1931), by Christian Walter v. Brunn, has been
made. The contents are classified, and music and music literature are to be
found in volume 1. The supplement to this work, for the years 1831 to 1840,
was compiled by H. Ehrencron-Müller (4 vols.; København: Gads, 1943-48).
Norwegian coverage for 1643 to 1813 is provided through Hjalmar Pettersen's
*Bibliotheca Norvegica* (4 vols.; Christiania: Cammayer, 1899-1924).
Bibliographical control for Sweden, in chronological order, is provided
through the *Sveriges bibliografi intill år 1600,* of Isak Collijn (3 vols.;
Uppsala: Svenska Litteratursällskapet, 1927-38), the *Sveriges bibliografi
1600-talet* (2 vols.; Uppsala: Almqvist, 1942-46), Hjalmar Linnström's
*Svenskt boklexikon åren 1830-65* (2 vols.; Stockholm: Linnström, 1883-84),
and the *Svensk bok-katalog för åren 1866-* (Stockholm: Tidningsaktiebolaget
Svensk Bokhandel, 1878-), the last listing both "Musik" and "Musikalier."
A rather extensive chronology of Finnish book production is provided in the

*Suomalainen Kirjallisuus* [1544-1939/43] (with supplements; Helsinki: Suomalaisen Kirjallisuuden Seura, 1878-1952). Rather comprehensive Swiss listings are found in Frédéric Charles Lonchamp's *Bibliographie générale des ouvrages publiés ou illustrés en Suisse et à l'étranger de 1475 à 1914 par des écrivains et des artistes suisses* (Paris et Lausanne: Librairie des Bibliophiles, 1922).

For Italy, Nicola Haym, *Biblioteca italiana, ossia Notizia de' libri rari italiani* (4 vols.; Milano: G. Silvestri, 1803) covers various periods. Two further sets are Attilio Pagliaini, *Catalogo generale della libreria italiana* [1847-99] (6 vols.; Milano: Assoc. Tip. Libr. Ital., 1901-22), of which new supplements bring coverage into the twentieth century, and *Bollettino delle pubblicazioni italiane* [1866-1957] (Firenze: Biblioteca Nazionale Centrale, 1886-1957). In the latter publication the classified index includes "Testi musicali."

Three Spanish sets may be consulted for retrospective bibliography. The first of these is the *Bibliografía española* (22 vols.; Madrid: Associación de la Librería, 1901-22). This lists music. Its continuations are the *Bibliografía general española e hispano-americana* (16 vols.; Madrid-Barcelona: Cámeras oficiales del libro, 1923-42) and the *Bibliografía hispanica* (16 vols.; Madrid: Instituto Nacional de Libro Español, 1942-57). Portuguese coverage for the fifteenth to the nineteenth centuries is found in Innocenzia Francisco da Silva, *Diccionario bibliográphico portuguez* (22 vols.; Lisboa: Impr. Nacional, 1858-1923).

EASTERN EUROPE—Two works by Karol Estreicher bring Polish coverage into the nineteenth century, the *Bibliografia polska* [1455-1880] (Krakow: Czcionkami Drukarni Universytetu Jagiellońskiego, 1870-) and the *Bibliografia polska 19. stulecia* (4 vols.; Kraków: Spólka Księgarzy Polsk., 1906-16), which is going through a second edition. Russian retrospective bibliography is extremely fragmented, but titles can be found in the bibliographies mentioned at the beginning of this chapter or in Winchell's *Guide.*

In Czechoslovakia the following years are covered by these respective publications: fifteenth century-1800, *Knihopis českých a slovenských tiskŭ* (Praha: [various publishers], 1925-); 1922-38, *Bibliografický katalog* (7 vols.; Praha: Nakladem vlastnim-Tiskl "Melantrich," 1923-28); and 1929-46, *Bibliografický katalog Československé Republiky* (18 vols.; V Praze: Nákladem Ministerstva Školství a Národní Osvěty, 1930-47). Hungarian bibliography for the fifteenth to the eighteenth centuries can be examined in Károly Szabó, *Régi magyar könyvtár* (3 vols.; Budapest: Tud, 1879-98), and for the period 1712-1910 we possess Géza Petrik, *Bibliographia hungarica* (11 vols.; Budapest: [various publishers], 1885-1942). Rumanian bibliography is provided through Ioan Bianu, Nerva Hodos and

EASTERN EUROPE *(Continued)*–Dan Simonescu, *Bibliografia românească veche 1508-1830* (4 vols.; Bucureşti: Atelierele, 1903-43). A century of Bulgarian coverage is provided in Aleksandr Téodorov-Balan's *Bŭlgarski knigopis za sto godini 1806-1905* (Sofia: Drzhavna Pechanitsa, 1909).

Emile Legrand has published the *Bibliographie hellénique* (4 vols., 1885-1906; 5 vols., 1894-1903; 2 vols., 1918-28; Paris: [various publishers]). This set, whose titles vary, covers Greek book production from the fifteenth to the eighteenth centuries. Bibliographical control over Albanian literary production is provided through Emile Legrand's *Bibliographie albanaise* [fifteenth century to 1900] (Paris: Welter, 1912) and Henry Gûys's title of the same name (Tirana: [no publisher], 1938), which covers the period 1900-1910.

Before closing, mention should be made of the series published by the U.S. Library of Congress, Slavic and Central European Division. The series is organized on a national basis and covers such items as books, abbreviations, periodicals, and other material.

# CHAPTER IV / Dictionaries

ALTHOUGH THE FOLLOWING CHAPTER is designed to offer a listing of those dictionaries normally required in the work of the music scholar, there are some titles which had to be excluded because of space limitations. Such dictionaries may be found in Robert L. Collison, *Dictionaries of Foreign Languages* (New York: Hafner, 1955); *Foreign Language-English Dictionaries* (2 vols.; Washington: Library of Congress, 1955), of which volume 1 contains a three-page section on music; or Wolfram Zaunmüller, *Bibliographisches Handbuch der Sprachwörterbücher* (Stuttgart: Hiersemann, 1958). The *International Bibliography of Dictionaries* (4th ed.; Berlin: Verlag Documentation, 1969), despite the English title, concentrates largely on subject dictionaries, as expressed in its German title: *Internationale Bibliographie der Fachwörterbücher.* Strong representation is given to technology, science, and economics, but there is a general section on "Übersetzungstechnik und Übersetzungsmaschinen."

Because of the growing importance of the Slavic languages in historical research, note should be made of Richard C. Lewanski, *A Bibliography of Slavic Dictionaries* (3 vols.; New York: New York Public Library, 1959-63). The general organization of the work is by monolingual, bilingual, and polyglot dictionaries, with subject indexes for each section.

## English Dictionaries

Two standard unabridged American dictionaries are *Webster's Third New International Dictionary of the English Language* (3rd ed.; Springfield, Mass.: Merriam, 1961) and *Funk and Wagnalls New "Standard" Dictionary of the English Language* (New York: Funk & Wagnalls, 1960).

The monumental dictionary of the English language is Sir James A. H. Murray's *New English Dictionary on Historical Principles* (10 vols., with supplement and bibliography; Oxford: Clarendon Press, 1888-1933), sometimes known as the "Oxford English Dictionary." The American counterpart is the *Dictionary of American English on Historical Principles* (4 vols.; Chicago: University of Chicago Press, 1936-44).[1]

## Foreign Language Dictionaries

In the following section, under countries or languages treated, the dictionary in that language is first listed, followed by the bilingual dictionary to English. In the former category the reference is usually to a historical rather than to a modern dictionary.

HEBREW AND THE CLASSICAL LANGUAGES—The monumental work for Hebrew is Eliezer Ben-Yehudah's *Thesaurus totius Hebraitatis et vetere et recentioris* (16 vols.; Berlin-Schöneberg: Langenscheidt, [1950-58]), which gives equivalents in English. For Greek Henri Estienne's *Thesaurus graecae linguae* (8 vols.; Paris: Didot, 1831-65) is very useful. Bilingual dictionaries of Hebrew and Greek, respectively, are Wilhelm Genesius, *Hebrew and English Lexicon of the Old Testament, with an Appendix Containing the Biblical Aramaic* (Oxford: Clarendon Press, 1952) and Henry G. Liddell and Robert Scott, *A Greek-English Lexicon* (new ed., with supplement; Oxford Clarendon Press, 1925-68).

Latin lexicography presents several facets. For classical Latin we have the *Thesaurus linguae latinae* (Lipsiae: Teubner, 1900-) and the new *Oxford Latin Dictionary* (Oxford: Clarendon Press, 1968-). Bilingual service is provided through Ethan Allen Andrews, *A Latin Dictionary . . . Revised, Enlarged and in Great Part Rewritten by Charlton T. Lewis and Charles Short* (Oxford: Clarendon Press, 1955 impression of the first edition of 1879), also known as *Harper's Latin Dictionary*. Charles Du Fresne Du Cange's *Glossarium mediae et infimae latinitatis* (10 vols., ed. nova; Niort: Favre, 1883-87) is the recognized authority in the field of medieval Latin. A bilingual dictionary of medieval Latin is Ronald E. Latham, *Revised Medieval Latin Word-List from British and Irish Sources* (London: Oxford University Press, 1965). In her *Latin for Local History* (New York: Longmans, 1961), Eileen E. Gooder provides typical documents with translations as well as a select word list. The church-music historian may find the *Dictionary of Liturgical Latin* (Milwaukee: Bruce, 1961), by Wilfred Diamond, or the *Kirchenlateinisches Wörterbuch* of Albert Sleumer (2. Auflage; Limburg: Steffen, 1926) of considerable help. The former provides over eleven thousand words from the Scriptures, the Breviary, the Missal, and similar sources.

---

[1] In their article "The Mystery of the Horn Papers," *The William and Mary Quarterly*, 3rd ser., IV (1947), 430-31, Arthur F. Middleton and Douglass Adair utilized these two historical dictionaries to investigate certain anachronistic words and phrases employed in a historical document.

WESTERN EUROPEAN LANGUAGES—Two larger French dictionaries are Robert Paul's *Dictionnaire alphabetique et analogique de la langue française* (6 vols.; Paris: Société du Nouveau Littré, 1960-64), sponsored by the Academie Française, and the older *Dictionnaire de la langue française* (7 vols., éd. integrale; Paris: Pauvert, 1956-58), by Émile Littré. *Heath's Standard French and English Dictionary* (2 vols., with supplement; New York: Heath, 1947-61), the British edition of which is entitled *Harrap's Standard French and English Dictionary*, is a reliable work for the English-speaking student.

The standard set for early German is Jacob and Wilhelm Grimm, *Deutsches Wörterbuch* (16 vols.; Leipzig: Hirzel, 1854-1960), of which a new edition is in progress (since 1965). Two bilingual dictionaries are Eduard Muret and Daniel Sanders, *Muret-Sanders enzyklopädisches englisch-deutsches und deutsch-englisches Wörterbuch* (2 vols., new ed. 1962-; Berlin-Schöneberg: Langenscheidt, 1908-33) and Harold T. Betteridge, *The New Cassell's German Dictionary; German-English, English-German* (New York: Funk & Wagnalls, 1958), the latter being a new edition of the well-known dictionary of Karl Breul.

Two very good Dutch dictionaries are Eelco Verwijs and Jacob Verdam, *Middelnederlandsch Woordenboek* ('s Gravenhage: Nijhoff, 1885-1952) and *Woordenboek der Nederlandsche Taal* ('s Gravenhage: Nijhoff, 1882-). In the absence of a Flemish dictionary for historical purposes the former may be used very effectively. The English-speaking person may consult H. Jansonius' *Groot Nederlands-Engels woordenboek voor studie en practijk* (2 vols.; Leiden: Nederlandsche uitgevermaatschappij n. v., 1950).

The historical dictionary for the Danish language is Verner Dahlerup, *Ordbog over det danske Sprog* (27 vols.; København: Gyldendal, 1919-54), although coverage does not reach back earlier than the seventeenth century. A highly recommended bilingual dictionary is the *Dansk-Engelsk Ordbog* (2 vols., 2nd ed.; København: Gyldendal, 1966), by Hermann Vinterberg and Carl Adolf Bodelsen. For the Norwegian language a monumental work, which reflects modern rather than historical usage, however, is the *Norsk riksmålordbok* by Trygve Knudsen and Alf Sommerfelt (2 vols.; Oslo: Aschehoug, 1937-57). English-speaking readers are served by the *Norwegian English Dictionary* (Madison: University of Wisconsin Press, [1965]), which is directed to American students.

Medieval Swedish is recorded in Knut Fredrik Söderwall's *Ordbok öfver svenska medeltids-språket* (2 vols.; Lund: Berlingska Boktryckeri, 1884-1918), whereas more recent usage may be found in the *Ordbok öfver svenska språket utgifven av Svenska Akademien* (Lund: [various publishers, 1898]). For bilingual use there exists Walter E. Harlock, *Svensk-engelsk ordbok* (2nd ed.; Stockholm: Svenska Bokförlaget, 1947). A monumental work for Finland is the *Suomalaisen Kirjallisuuden Seura* (6 vols.; Porvoo: Söderstrom, 1957-62), while a very fine bilingual dictionary is V. S. Alanne, *Suomalaisen englantilainen sanakirja* (2nd ed.; Porvoo: Söderstrom, 1962).

A comprehensive dictionary of Italian is the *Vocabolario degli Accademici della Crusca* (11 vols., A-O, 5. impressione; Firenze: Cellini, 1863-1923), which will probably be superseded by Salvatore Battaglia, *Grande dizionario della lingua italiane* (Torino: UTET, 1961-), a very scholarly work. For bilingual purposes Alfred Hoare's *Italian Dictionary* (2nd ed.; Cambridge: The University Press, 1925) may be highly recommended, although the reader may prefer to use the more modern *Cambridge Italian Dictionary* (Cambridge: University Press, 1962-), by Barbara Reynolds, for which specialists have been consulted.

In the area of the Spanish language the Academia España is sponsoring the *Diccionario histórico de la lengua española* (Madrid: Real Academia Española, 1960-), but because of the very slow rate of publication of this work the reader may wish to turn to Martín Alonso Pedraz' *Enciclopedia del idioma; Diccionario histórico y moderno de la lengua española* (3 vols.; Madrid: Aguilar, 1958). Bilingual coverage is provided in Mariano Velázquez de la Cadena, *New Revised Velázquez Spanish and English Dictionary* (2 vols., rev. ed.; Chicago: Follett, [1961]). The Portuguese language is represented by António de Moraes e Silva's *Grande dicionário da lingua portuguesa* (12 vols., 10th ed.; Lisboa: Ed. Confluéncia, 1949-59) and J. Albino Ferreira, *Dicionário inglês-português, português-inglês* (2 vols., nova ed.; Oporto: Barreira, 1952-54), in the latter of which Brazilian terms may also be found.

EASTERN EUROPEAN LANGUAGES.—A work which extends to ancient as well as to modern Greek is the *Mega lexikon tēs hellēnikēs glōssēs* (9 vols.; Athens: Dēmētrakou, 1936-50). For Albania there exists a work which is at once historical and bilingual, albeit of only one volume, the *Historical Albanian and English Dictionary* [1496-1938] (London: Longmans, 1948), by Stuart E. Mann.

Languages spoken in Yugoslavia are Serbo-Croatian and Slovenian. Dictionaries for the former language are the *Rječnik hrvatskoga ili srpskoga jezika* (19 vols.; U Zagrebu: U Knižarnici L. Hartmana, 1880-1967) and *An English-Serbocroatian Dictionary* (Belgrade: "Prosveta," 1962). A historical dictionary for Slovenian is being issued by the Slovenian Academy under the title *Slovar slovenskega knjižnega jezika* (Ljubljana: Slovenska Akademija Znanosti in Umetnosti, 1970-), while the *Slovensko-angleški slovar* (6th ed.; Ljubljana: Državna Založba Slovenije, 1967), of Janko Kotnik, serves for translating purposes.

The language lexicography for Rumania consists of the *Dicţionarul limbii române* (Bucareşti: [various publishers], 1913-, continued by the *Serie novă*), which gives archaisms and forms of a regional nature, and the *Dicţionar Român-Englez* (2nd ed.; Bucareşti: Editura Ştiinţifică, 1965), by Leon Leviţchi. Two complementary works for Hungary are Gábor Szárvas and Zsigmond Simonyi, *Lexicon linguae hungaricae aevi antiquioris* (3 vols.; Budapest: Hornyánszky, 1890-93), which is the historical dictionary of the Hungarian Academy of Sciences, and the *Hungarian-English Dictionary* by László Országh (2 vols., 3rd ed.; Budapest: Akadémiai Kiadó, 1969).

The Czech Academy has sponsored the *Přívční slovník jazyka českého* (8 vols.; Praha: Státní Pedagogické Nakladatelství, 1935-57), while the *English-Czech and Czech-English Dictionary* (16th ed.; Prague: Orbis, 1959), of Jindřich Procházka, is an up-to-date bilingual guide for the Czech language. The Slovak language is represented by the *Slovník slovenského jazyka* (5 vols.; Bratislava: Vydavateľstvo Slovenskej Akadémie Vied, 1959-65), sponsored by the Slovakian Academy, or, for translation purposes, by *Hrobak's English Slovak Dictionary* (2nd ed.; New York: Speller, [1965]), compiled by Philip A. Hrobak.

The dictionary for the older state of the Polish language is the *Słownik staropolski* (Warszawa: Polska Akademia Nauk, 1953-), still in process of publication, while Jan Stanisławski's *Great English-Polish Dictionary* (Warszawa: State Publishing House, 1964) may be effectively used by English-speaking readers.

A recent edition of the monumental Russian dictionary of Vladimir Ivanovich Dal' is *Tolkovyĭ slovar' zhivogo velikorusskogo iazyka* (4 vols., 6th ed.; Moskva: Izdtvo Inostrannykh i Natsional'nykh Slovarei, 1955). For bilingual use the *Russian-English Dictionary* by Aleksandr Ivanovich Smirnitskii has gone through a third edition by O. S. Akhmanova (New York: Dutton, 1959). Two dictionaries of note for Bulgarian are Stefan Mladenov and A. T. Balan, *Bŭlgarski tŭlkoven rechnik* (Sofia: "Decho Stefanov," 1951-) and Gocho G. Chakalov's *Bŭlgarsko-angliĭski rechnik* (Sofia: Nayka i izkustvo, 1961).

## Special Terminological Dictionaries

For bibliographical and documentary investigation valuable assistance is provided by Leonard M. Harrod's *The Librarian's Glossary; Terms Used in Librarianship and the Book Crafts* (2nd ed.; London: Grafton, 1959) or by Philip H. Vitale's *Bibliography, Historical and Bibliothecal; A Handbook of Terms and Names* (Chicago: Loyala University Press, 1971). English, French, German, Spanish, and Russian library terms are presented in Anthony Thompson's *Vocabularium bibliothecarii* (2nd ed.; [no place] UNESCO, 1962), with an index in each language.

The *Adeline Art Dictionary* (New York: Ungar, [1966]), by Jules Adeline, provides terms used in art, architecture, heraldry, and archeology, and has been brought up to date by a supplement written by Hugo G. Beigel. Two dictionaries will be of aid to the opera specialist; these are *Theatre Language; A Dictionary of Terms in English of the Drama and Stage from Medieval to Modern Times* (New York: Theatre Arts, 1961), by Walter P. Bowman and Robert Hamilton, and the *Lexique international de termes techniques de théâtre en huit langues* (New York: Theatre Arts Books, [1959]). The latter provides American, Dutch, English, German, Italian, Spanish, and Swedish terms.

Ancillary aids for the music historian include Eugen Haberkern and Joseph Friedrich Wallach, *Hilfswörterbuch für Historiker; Mittelalter und Neuzeit* (2. Auflage; Bern: Francke, 1964) and the *Longmans Dictionary of Geography* (London: Longmans, 1966). In the former title the emphasis is on the Latin, German, and French languages, but the second edition does reflect political changes in Eastern Europe.

Music scholars with text-related problems have two terminological resources. These are Arthur Finley Scott's *Current Literary Terms; A Concise Dictionary of Their Origin and Use* (New York: St. Martin's Press, 1965) and Mario Andrew Pei, *Glossary of Linguistic Terminology* (New York: Columbia University Press, 1966). Babette Deutsch's *Poetry Handbook; A Dictionary of Terms* (3rd ed.; New York: Funk & Wagnalls, [1961]) contains a long and informative article on "Metre" as well as coverage of such terms as "Rondel" and "Terza rima."

Clement S. Mihanovich, Robert J. McNamara, and William N. Tome have published a *Glossary of Sociological Terms* (Milwaukee: Bruce, [1967]), which provides some foreign equivalents as well as a glossary index. *The Dictionary of Statistical Terms* (2nd ed.; New York: Hafner, 1960), by Maurice G. Kendall and William R. Buckland, provides not only the basic dictionary in English, but also glossaries in French, German, Italian, and Spanish, with particular strength in Italian. The ethnomusicologist may make advantageous use of Charles Winick's *Dictionary of Anthropology* (New York: Philosophical Library, 1956).

Although most authors utilizing abbreviations to any extent usually give lists of such in the body of the work, occasional reference to dictionaries of abbreviations may be necessary. Of the many available, two English-language dictionaries which lean toward the humanities are Frank D. Fawcett's *Cyclopedia of Initials and Abbreviations* (London: Business Publications, 1963) and Robert J. Schwartz's *The Complete Dictionary of Abbreviations* (New York: Crowell, 1955). Dictionaries of French and German abbreviations, respectively, are Hubert Baudry, *"D. A." Dictionnaire d'abréviations françaises et étrangères, techniques et usuelles, anciennes et nouvelles* (La Chapelle-Montligeon: Ed. de Montligeon, 1951) and Josef Greiser, *Lexikon der Abkürzungen* (2. Auflage; Osnabrück: Fromm, 1955). Alex A. Kramer's

*Sokrashcheniia v sovetskikh izdaniiakh* ([Trenton, N.J.: Scientific Russian Translating Service, 1965]) not only resolves Russian abbreviations, but also provides translations.

Before closing this chapter, four further resources should be mentioned. These are Carter V. Good's *Dictionary of Education* (New York: McGraw-Hill, 1959); James Drever's *Dictionary of Psychology* ([rev. ed.] ; Baltimore: Penguin Books, 1964); *Chambers's Technical Dictionary* (3rd ed.; New York: Macmillan, 1958); and Harold A. Rodgers' *Funk & Wagnalls Dictionary of Data Processing Terms* (New York: Funk & Wagnalls, [1970]), the last-named aiding scholars interested in research through use of the computer and data processing.

A BIBLIOGRAPHICAL GUIDE to encyclopedias which is also strongly historical is Robert Collison, *Encyclopedias: Their History Throughout the Ages* (2nd ed.; New York: Hafner, 1966). Coverage begins with the year 350 B.C., and the approach is chronological. Gert A. Zischka's *Index Lexicorum; Bibliographie der lexikalischen Nachschlagewerke* (New York: Hafner, 1959) lists first general encyclopedias and following this continues with a subject orientation.

Two works by S. Padraigh Walsh serve as encyclopedia bibliographies. The first of these, *Anglo-American General Encyclopedias; A Historical Bibliography, 1703-1967* (New York: Bowker, 1968) lists 419 English-language encyclopedias by title, whereas the second, *General Encyclopedias in Print 1968; A Comprehensive Analysis* (New York: Bowker, 1968), gives ratings and is largely consumer-oriented.

## General Encyclopedias

*The Encyclopedia Americana* (30 vols., [1965 ed.] ; New York: Americana Corporation, [1965]) contains signed articles by specialists. It is supplemented by the *Americana Annual.* Some indication of scope may be gained from the length of the article "Beethoven" (seven columns). The *Collier's Encyclopaedia* (24 vols.; New York and Toronto: Crowell, Collier and Macmillan, 1966) contains signed articles by authorities. The article on "Music, History of," by Victor Yellin, is forty-three pages in length. The *1968 Yearbook of Facts on File; A Weekly World News Digest* (New York: Facts on File, 1940-) includes the heading "Music," with subheadings for "Awards," "Books Published," "Obituaries," "Opera," "Phonograph Records," and "Symphonies," as well as further headings for "Musicians." Quinquennial indexes have been published from 1946 on. A good quick reference guide is the one-volume *Columbia Encyclopedia* (3rd ed.; New York: Columbia University Press, 1963).

Outstanding sets also include, of course, the distinguished *Encyclopaedia Britannica* (24 vols.; Chicago: Encyclopaedia Britannica, c1964). The articles are signed, and the specialist for music is Gerald E. H. Abraham, with Nicholas Slonimsky representing American music. The edition is supplemented by the *Britannica Book of the Year.* Among British sets, the scholarly *Chambers's Encyclopaedia* has recently been published in a new revised edition (16 vols.; Oxford: Pergamon Press, c1967). Departmental adviser for music is Frank S. Howes. A relative newcomer to the scene is the *Encyclopedia Canadiana* (10 vols.; Ottawa: Canadiana Co., 1957-58).

The French encyclopedist Pierre Larousse has been the originator of a monumental series, within which are the *Grand dictionnaire universel du XIXe siècle français* (17 vols.; Paris: Larousse, [1865-90] ); the *Larousse du XXe siècle . . . publié sous la direction de Paul Augé* (6 vols.; Paris: Larousse, c1928-33), with a supplement published in 1953; and the *Larousse mensuel illustré* (14 vols.; Paris: Larousse, 1907-57), which is a monthly supplement of the *Nouveau Larousse illustré* (8 vols.; 1898-1907). New additions to the list are the *Grand Larousse encyclopédique* (10 vols. and supplement; Paris: Larousse, 1960-[68] ), among whose musical contributors are Jacques Chailley, Suzanne Clercx-Lejeune, Armand Machabey, Marc Pincherle, and Charles van den Borren, and *La Grande Encyclopédie* (Paris: Larousse, 1971-), with contributions by Norbert Dufourcq and Marc Pincherle. Also to be mentioned is the authoritative *Grande encyclopédie; Inventaire raisonné des sciences, des lettres et des arts* (31 vols.; Paris: Lamirault, 1886-1902). Historical subjects receive particularly thorough treatment here.

The latest edition of the venerable German "Brockhaus" is entitled *Brockhaus Enzyklopädie in zwanzig Bänden* (17. Auflage; Wiesbaden: Brockhaus, 1966-). The set is particularly valuable for arriving at Slavic place names used today for the German place names found in the earlier literature (e.g., Pressburg/Bratislava). An adjunct German lexicographical work is *Meyers neues Lexikon in acht Bänden* (Leipzig: VEB Bibliographisches Institut, 1961-).

For Italy the *Enciclopedia italiana di scienze, lettere ed arti* (36 vols. plus supplements; Roma: Istituto Treccani, 1929-39) is of importance. A subsequent publication is the *Dizionario enciclopedico italiano* (12 vols.; Roma: Istituto della Enciclopedia Italiana, 1955-61). The articles in the former are signed, while those of the latter set are shorter and not signed.

The Spanish "Espasa," *Enciclopedia universal illustrada Europeo-Americana* (80 vols.; Barcelona: Espasa, 1905-33) is very comprehensive and good in its music coverage. "Annual" supplements have been issued since 1934. The monumental Russian *Bol'shaia sovetskaia entsiklopediia* (51 vols. plus indexes, 2nd ed.; Moskva: Izd-vo Bolshaia Sovetskaia Entsiklopediia, 1950-58) is maintained by an annual *Ezhegodnik,* but a third edition is in progress.

## Notes and Queries

Odd bits of information can sometimes be gathered through the type of publication known as "Notes and Queries." The quality of indexing, which is particularly important for this type of journal, varies a great deal in the respective series.

An early serial of this nature is the British *Notes and Queries; A Medium of Intercommunication for Literary Men* (London: [various publishers], 1850-). The frequency varies. General indexes are issued.

The French version is *Intermédiaire des chercheurs et curieux* (103 vols.; Paris: [various publishers], 1864-1940). This has a subject index in each volume. Its successor is *L'Intermédiaire des chercheurs et curieux* (Paris: Chercheurs et Curieux, 1951-), which is issued monthly.

The *American Notes and Queries; A Journal for the Curious* (8 vols.; [place varies]: American Notes and Queries, 1941-50) is provided with annual and quinquennial cumulated indexes. Its successor is *American Notes and Queries* (New Haven: American Notes and Queries, 1962-), which provides annual cumulated indexes.

## Special Encyclopedias

Two encyclopedias devoted to library science have been published in recent years. These are the *Encyclopedia of Librarianship* (3rd ed.; London: Bowes & Bowes, 1966), compiled by Thomas Landau, and the *Encyclopedia of Library and Information Science* (New York: Marcel Dekker, 1968-). The former includes a very informative article on "Music Libraries," by John Howard Davies, reflecting the British viewpoint. A cognate work to these is Joachim Kirchner's *Lexikon des Buchwesens* (2 vols.; Stuttgart: Hiersemann, 1952-53), which provides articles on "Musikbibliographie," "Musikbücher," "Musikhandschriften," "Musik-Erstausgaben," "Musiknotendruck," and "Musikverlag."

The monumental work for classical studies is August Friedrich von Pauly, *Paulys Real-Encyclopädie der classischen Altertumswissenschaft* (Neue Bearbeitung; Stuttgart: Metzler, 1894-), which includes signed articles and bibliographies. For quick reference the reader may use the *Oxford Classical Dictionary* (Oxford: Clarendon Press, 1949) or the *New Century Classical Handbook,* edited by Catherine B. Avery (New York: Appleton-Century-Crofts, 1962). The scholar interested in Byzantine music or its influence on western music may well find Paul Wirth's *Reallexikon der Byzantinistik* (Amsterdam: Hakkert, 1968-) of considerable aid.

Subjects pertaining to religion are covered in the *Encyclopaedia of Religion and Ethics* (13 vols.; New York: Scribner, 1908-27). For the Catholic Church

important reference sets are the *Catholic Encyclopedia* (17 vols.; New York:
Catholic Encyclopedia Press, [1907-22]), of which a revised edition of
volume 1 was published by the Gilmary Society in New York in 1936, and
the *New Catholic Encyclopedia* (15 vols.; New York: McGraw-Hill, 1967).
For the latter work the music editor was the Rt. Rev. Rembert G. Weakland,
O.S.B., while contributors of signed articles on music include E. Gerson-Kiwi,
G. Reese, and T. Georgiades. An Italian counterpart to these publications is
the *Enciclopedia cattolica* (12 vols.; Città del Vaticano: Enciclopedia Cattolica,
1948-54). Two German encyclopedias are the *Lexikon für Theologie und
Kirche* (10 vols., 2. Auflage; Freiburg: Herder, 1957-65), by Michael Buchberger,
and *Die Religion in Geschichte und Gegenwart* (6 vols., 3. Auflage; Tübingen:
Mohr, 1957-62), the latter Protestant oriented. For ritual, customs, and
history of the church two works to be consulted are Fernand Cabrol, Henri
Leclercq, and Henri Marrou, *Dictionnaire d'archéologie chrétienne et de liturgie*
(15 vols.; Paris: Letouzey, 1907-53), covering the period to roughly 800 A.D.,
and the *Enciclopedia ecclesiastica* (Milano: Vallardi, 1942-). Two works
detailing the importance of such matters as orders and geographical locations
in the life of the Roman Catholic Church are Pierre Helyot, *Dictionnaire des
ordres religieux* (4 vols.; Paris: Migne, 1859-63) and Alfred Baudrillart,
*Dictionnaire d'histoire et de géographie ecclésiastiques* (17 vols.; Paris: Letouzey
et Ané, 1912-69), the latter including information on musicians associated with
the Church. The Helyot work is part of a vast series by J. P. Migne entitled
*Encyclopédie théologique* (168 vols.; Paris: Migne, 1845-73), a series which
includes dictionaires covering various ecclesiastical subjects. The *Lutheran
Encyclopedia* (St. Louis, Mo.: Concordia, 1954) is an example of the many
fine handbooks issued by various Protestant denominations.

Three works dealing with Jewish subjects are the *Encyclopaedia Judaica;
Das Judentum in Geschichte und Gegenwart* (10 vols.; Berlin: Eschkol,
1928-34), the *Encyclopaedia Judaica* (16 vols.; New York: Macmillan, 1971),
and the *Universal Jewish Encyclopedia* (10 vols.; New York: Universal Jewish
Encyclopedia, 1939-44). References to Islamic subjects are to be found in the
*Encyclopaedia of Islam* (new ed.; Leiden: Brill, 1954-).

Aids to the music scholar in the area of the arts include the *Encyclopedia of
World Art* (15 vols.; New York: McGraw-Hill, 1959-68) and the *Enciclopedia
dello spettacolo* (9 vols. plus appendixes; Roma: Le Maschera, 1954-66).
Motion picture arts are represented in the latter publication as well as in the
*Filmlexicon degli autori e delle opere* (Roma: Bianco e Nero, 1958-), whose
section 1 includes composers.

The universal approach with no chronological restriction is demonstrated in
the *Encyclopedia of Philosophy* (8 vols.; New York: Macmillan, [1967]), which
contains signed articles with bibliographies. For reference in the field of history
the musicologist may want to consult *An Encyclopedia of World History* (4th

rev. ed.; Boston: Houghton, 1968), by William H. Langer. While being essentially a literature encyclopedia, the *Dizionario di tutte le letterature* ([Milano] : Bompiani, 1947–) is strong in music.

Music contributors to the *International Encyclopedia of the Social Sciences* (17 vols.; [New York] : Macmillan, [c1968]) include Alan P. Merriam and Hans Engel. It is particularly strong in the fields of the sociology of music, ethnomusicology, and the psychology of music. The *Handbuch der Psychologie in 12 Bänden* (Göttingen: Verlag für Psychologie, [1959–]) contains signed articles with bibliographies. Music is found in volume 6, together with several subheadings, in the *Encyclopedia of Education* (10 vols.; New York: Macmillan, 1971). The *McGraw-Hill Encyclopedia of Science and Technology* (15 vols., [rev. ed.] ; New York: McGraw-Hill, [1966]) is updated from 1962 by the *McGraw-Hill Yearbook of Science and Technology*.

# CHAPTER VI / Biography

## Indexes and Bibliographies

A recent comprehensive bibliography of works conveying biographical information is Robert B. Slocum's *Biographical Dictionaries and Related Works* (Detroit: Gale Research, c1967). This is an annotated volume containing sections on "Universal Biography," "National or Area Biography," and "Biography by Vocation." Music occupies 392 entries. Areas within countries, such as "Rhone" or "Baden," are included.

The purpose of a biographical index or of a bibliography of biography is to guide the reader to biographical information which may be found in periodicals, books, or series. Three such works are Phyllis M. Riches, *Analytical Bibliography of Universal Collected Biography* (London: Library Association, 1934), Albert M. Hyamson, *A Dictionary of Universal Biography of All Ages and of All Peoples* (2nd ed.; New York: Dutton, 1951), and Max Arnim, *Internationale Personal-bibliographie, 1800–1959* (3 vols., 2. Auflage; Leipzig: Hiersemann, 1944–63). The last is particularly valuable from a bio-bibliographical standpoint. To these may be added a work important for its coverage of the older literature, Eduard M. Oettinger's *Bibliographie biographique universelle* (2 vols.; Bruxelles: Stienon, 1854).

A serials publication of a comprehensive nature is the *Biography Index; A Cumulative Index to Biographical Material in Books and Magazines* [1946–] (New York: Wilson, 1947–). The *Biography Index* appears quarterly, with annual and triennial cumulations.

Two specialized indexes are of particular interest to the historian. The first of these is Cyr Ulysse Chevalier's *Répertoire des sources historiques du moyen âge; Bio-bibliographie* (2 vols., nouv. éd.; Paris: Picard, 1903–7), which is a companion to his *Topo-bibliographie* (2 vols.; 1894–1903). The second of these is the *Dictionnaire des noms, surnoms, et pseudonymes latins de l'histoire littéraire du moyen age [1100 à 1530]* (Paris: Firmin-Didot, 1875), by Alfred L. A. Franklin. Variant names are given in the articles and an "Index alphabeticus" indexes by the subject's Christian name.

Before closing this section mention should be made of *Biographical Sources for Foreign Countries* (4 parts; Washington: Library of Congress, 1944–45).

In part 1, a general section, there is a rubric for "Musicians," and in part 2, devoted to Germany and Austria, biographical sources for "Music" are given.

## International Biographical Dictionaries

Two somewhat parallel French works may head the list of international biographies. These are "Michaud," that is, *Biographie universelle, ancienne et moderne* (45 vols., nouv. éd.; Paris: Desplaces, 1843-65), and "Hoefer," the *Nouvelle biographie générale* (46 vols.; Paris: Didot, 1853-66). A dictionary with shorter articles is that by Eduard M. Oettinger, *Moniteur des dates; Biographisch-genealogisch-historisches Welt-Register* (9 vols; Leipzig: [various publishers], 1869-82), with over one hundred thousand entries.

From the twentieth century, and therefore containing more current information, is Pierre Grimal's *Dictionnaire des biographies* (2 vols.; Paris: Presses universitaires des France, 1958). In *The New Century Cyclopedia of Names* (3 vols.; New York: Appleton-Century-Crofts, 1954), Beethoven receives nearly two columns. The *World Biography* (New York: Institute for Research in Biography, 1940-) gives not only short biographical sketches, but also business or office addresses.

*Current Biography; Who's News and Why* (New York: Wilson, 1940-), a monthly publication with annual cumulations, gives full biographies of living persons on the contemporary scene.

## National Biographical Dictionaries

Collections of national biographies are legion in number. Only a selection of titles can be given here. Not included in this list, but published in many countries of the world, are "Who's Who" volumes for contemporary persons. The scholar should also be aware of genealogical guides to the nobility, such as the *Almanach de Gotha* (Gotha: Perthes, 1764-), *Burke's Genealogical and Heraldic History of the Peerage, Baronetage, and Knightage* (London: [various publishers], 1826-), and J. B. P. J. de Courcelles, *Dictionnaire universel de la noblesse de France* (5 vols.; Paris: Bureau Générale de la Noblesse de France, 1820-22). Historical research is also often served by published matriculation records of older universities such as Oxford University's *Alumni Oxoniensis* (8 vols.; Oxford and London: Parker, 1888-92) or the University of Basle's *Die Matrikel der Universität Basel* (Basel: Universitätsbibliothek, 1951-). Obituaries, although represented in the following sections to only a limited extent, should not be overlooked as sources of biographical information. Slocum's volume is a guide to further titles in these categories.

THE UNITED STATES—Two bibliographical guides to American biography
are Marion Dargan, *Guide to American Biography* (Albuquerque:
University of New Mexico Press, 1949-) and Louis Kaplan, *A Bibliography
of American Autobiographies* (Madison: University of Wisconsin Press, 1961).
In the former the arrangement is chronological and geographical and in the
latter the index reflects "Musicians," with chronological subheadings.

The *National Cyclopaedia of American Biography* (New York: White,
1893-) is a very comprehensive work, but the indexes must be used to
approach the material. The *Dictionary of American Biography* (20 vols.,
plus supplements and index; New York: Scribner, 1928-37) is maintained
by supplements for five-year periods.

Of special importance to the academic world is the *Directory of American
Scholars* (4 vols., 5th ed.; New York: Cattell, 1969). Musicologists will be
found in volume 1 of the 1969 edition. Latest positions and addresses are
given. The *National Faculty Directory, 1970* (Detroit: Gale Research, 1970)
provides addresses for 320,000 faculty members of junior colleges, colleges,
and universities in the United States. Regional Who's Who volumes exist for
the United States, such as the *Who's Who in the Midwest* (Chicago: Marquis, 1949-).


BRITAIN AND THE BRITISH COMMONWEALTH—An index to older material is
provided by Sir William Musgrave's *Obituary Prior to 1800* (6 vols.; London:
Harleian Society, 1899-1901), which is of importance for England, Scotland,
and Ireland. Newer, and more comprehensive with regard to geographical
extent, is Donald H. Simpson's *Biography Catalogue of the Library of the
Royal Commonwealth Society* (London: Royal Commonwealth Society,
1961).

The classical set for Great Britain is the *Dictionary of National Biography*
(22 vols., index, and supplements; London: [various publishers], 1885-).
Only deceased persons are included. The articles are signed and contain very
good bibliographies. For quick reference the *Concise Dictionary* of this same
title may suffice (Oxford: Oxford University Press, 1903). For Scotland,
Ireland, and Wales we have William Anderson, *The Scottish Nation* (3 vols.;
Edinburgh: Fullarton, [1859]-63), John S. Crone, *A Concise Dictionary of
Irish Biography* (rev. and enlarged ed.; New York: Longmans, 1937), and
*The Dictionary of Welsh Biography Down to 1940* (Oxford: Blackwell,
1959), respectively.

The *Dictionary of Canadian Biography* (Toronto: University of Toronto
Press, [1966-]) and the *Australian Dictionary of Biography* ([Melbourne]:
Melbourne University Press, [1966-]) are two recent and very welcome
additions to the wealth of national biographical dictionaries. Both are based
on chronological organization.

WESTERN EUROPE—Two French dictionaries may be consulted. The first of these, retrospective in nature, is the *Dictionnaire de biographie française* (Paris: Letouzey, 1933-). Modern figures find mention in the *Dictionnaire biographique français contemporaine* (2. éd.; Paris: Pharos, [1954]).

The standard work for Germany is the *Allgemeine deutsche Biographie* (56 vols.; Leipzig: Duncker, 1875-1912), in which coverage of composers, performers, and even instrument makers is provided. Two later works are the *Neue deutsche Biographie* (Berlin: Duncker und Humblot, 1953-) and *Die grossen Deutschen; Deutsche Biographie* (4 vols.; Berlin: Propyläen-Verlag, [1956-57]), the latter by Hermann Heimpel, Theodor Heuss, and Benno Reifenberg. The German analogue to the *Directory of American Scholars* is *Kürschners deutscher Gelehrten-Kalender 1966* (2 vols., 10. Auflage; Berlin: De Gruyter, 1966), which lists German scholars in non-literary fields. The index by discipline includes "Musikwissenschaft," and there is a listing of "Wissenschaftliche Verlage" by country.

Prominent men and women of the Austro-Hungarian Empire, which at one time included such musically rich countries as Bohemia and Hungary, are covered in Constantin Wurzbach's *Biographisches Lexikon des Kaiserthums Oesterreich* [1750] (60 vols.; Wien: Zamarski, 1856-91). Later personages may be treated either in the *Neue österreichische Biographie* [1815-] (Wien: Amalthea-Verlag, 1923-) or in the *Österreichisches biographisches Lexikon* [1815-] (Graz-Köln: Böhlaus, 1954-), the latter sponsored by the Akademie der Wissenschaften.

Swiss figures are presented in the *Dictionnaire historique & biographique de la Suisse* (7 vols. and supplement; Neuchâtel: Administration du Dictionnaire historique et biographique de la Suisse, 1921-34), while Belgians of note are represented in the *Biographie nationale* (Bruxelles: [various publishers], 1866-) and its supplements, published by the Académie Royale des Sciences, des Lettres, et des Beaux-arts de Belgique. Persons of Flemish origin who are not to be found in the *Biographie nationale* may be listed in the *Nationaal biografisch woordenboek* (Brussel: Paleis der Academiën, 1964). The *Biographie nationale du pays de Luxembourg* (Luxembourg: Buck, 1947-) is not arranged in an alphabetical manner, but indexes are provided in each volume. Dutch notables may be found in the *Biographisch woordenboek der Nederlanden* (21 vols.; Haarlem: Brederode, 1852-78), compiled by Abraham Jacobus van der Aa, or in the *Nieuw Nederlandsch biografisch woordenboek* (10 vols.; Leiden: Sijthoff, 1911-37), compiled by P. C. Molhuysen. The older work places a particularly valuable emphasis on bibliography.

For Danish and Norwegian figures one may consult the *Dansk biografisk leksikon* (27 vols.; København: Schultz, 1933-44) and the *Norsk biografisk leksikon* (Oslo: Aschehoug, 1923-), respectively. Sweden is provided with the *Svenskt biografiskt lexikon* (Stockholm: Bonnier, 1917-), while for Finland the *Kansallinen elämäkerrasto* (5 vols.; Porvoo: Söderström, [1927-34]) serves as a national biography.

A recent Spanish set in progress is the *Diccionario biográfico español e hispanoamericano* (Palma de Mallorca: Instituto Español de Estudios Biográficos, 1950-). As the title implies, Spanish-American figures are also covered in this publication. A universal work which at the same time controls Portuguese biography is Theodore José da Silva's *Miscellanea historico-biographica* (Lisboa: [privately printed], 1877). The *Enciclopedia biografica e bibliografica "Italiana"* (Milano: Tosi, 1936-) is issued in a classified series. Another set in progress covering Italian persons is the *Dizionario biografico italiani* (Roma: Enciclopedia italiana, [1960-]).

EASTERN EUROPE—A biographical dictionary which serves for modern Greece is the *Mega Hellēnikon biographikon lexikon* ([Athens]: "Biomēchanikēs Epitheōrēseos" [1958-]). Yugoslavian persons of note are covered in the *Slovenski biografski leksikon* (Ljubljana: [various publishers], 1925-).

Hungarian authors are treated in the *Magyar irók; Elete és munkái* (Új sorozat; Budapest: Magyar Könyvtárosok és Leveltárosok Egyesülete, 1939-), by Pál Gulyás. A work published in Germany, the *Biographisches Handbuch der Tschechoslowakei* (Munchen: Lerche, 1961), by Heinrich Kuhn and Otto Böss, provides information about living persons. The biographical section is preceded by a systematic section. A set published by the Polish Akademja Umiejetności Kraków is the *Polski słownik biograficzny* (Kraków: Nakladem Polskiej Akademii Umiejetności, 1935-).

Several publications are of importance with regard to the Soviet Union. Bio-bibliography is brought under control through the *Russkie biographicheskie i bibliographicheskie slovari* (Moskva: Gos. izd—vo kul'turno-prosvet. lit-ry, 1955). An older set from the days of the empire is the *Russkiĭ biographicheskiĭ slovar'* (25 vols.; S.-Peterburg: [various publishers], 1896-1918). For later personages one should consult the *Biographic Directory of the USSR* (New York: Scarecrow, 1958). Before closing, mention should be made of a publication of the Slavic Seminar of the University of Munich, the *Kleine slavische Biographie* (Wiesbaden: Harrassowitz, 1958), which provides brief biographies for the entire Slavic region.

## Biographical Dictionaries by Vocation

Many dictionaries of prominent people arranged by vocation are so specialized or localized that mention of them here would go beyond the limits of this manual. The interested reader is referred to the volume by Slocum as a guide to such compendiums. Various of the special encyclopedias listed in Chapter V of the present work may also reveal biographical information within the fields covered. Certain rather general publications which, for one reason or another, lie rather close to scholarly endeavours in music are brought out in the following paragraphs.

Ecclesiastical figures are covered in Louis E. Dupin's *A New History of Ecclesiastical Writers* (13 vols.; London: Smalle and Childe, 1693-99) or in the *Acta sanctorum quotquot tot orbe coluntur* (editio novissima; Parisiis: Palmé, 1863-). The former includes literary individuals from the first age of the Church to the fifteenth century, while the latter is devoted to hagiography and is supplemented by certain volumes of the *Analecta bollandiana* from 1885 on. Figures such as troubadours find mention in *European Authors, 1000-1900; A Biographical Dictionary of European Literature* (New York: Wilson, 1967), by Stanley J. Kunitz and Vineta Colby. Writers of our own time are treated in *Contemporary Authors; A Bio-Bibliographical Guide to Current Authors and Their Works* (Detroit: Gale Research, 1962-), edited by James M. Etheridge. Eminent men and women in the field of education are found in Charles W. Bardeen's *A Dictionary of Educational Biography* (Syracuse: Bardeen, 1901), listing over four hundred portraits and sketches, or in the *Dictionary of Educationists* (London: Pitman, [1914]), by James E. Roscoe. Translators working in various parts of the world are given listings in Bob Pond's *International Directory of Translators and Interpreters* (London: Pond, 1967). Although there is no rubric for music, one is provided for "Arts."

Registers of early printers and publishers contribute considerably to our knowledge of early music typography. Examples of such accounts are the *Catalogue of Italian Publishers and Printers of the XVth Century* (Milan: Toscanini, 1930), by Mario Armanni; Ferdinand Geldner's *Die deutschen Inkunabeldrucker; Ein Handbuch der deutschen Buchdrucker des XV. Jahrhunderts nach Druckorten* (2 vols.; Stuttgart: Hiersemann, 1968-70); *Die Buchdrucker des 16. und 17. Jahrhunderts im deutschen Sprachgebiet* (Wiesbaden: Harrassowitz, 1963), by Josef Benzing; Georges Lepreux's *Gallia typographia* (7 vols.; Paris: Champion, 1909-14), listing French printers to the Revolution; and Edward G. Duff's *A Century of the English Book Trade* (London: Bibliographical Society, 1905), treating printers, stationers, bookbinders, and others connected with the trade from 1457 to 1557.

Finally, mention should be made of a handbook which may prove eminently valuable to those interested in music and the dramatic arts. This is Harold S. and Marjory Z. Sharp's *Index to Characters in the Performing Arts* (New York: Scarecrow, 1966-), of which part 2 covers operas and musical productions.

## Anonyms and Pseudonyms

Dictionaries which reveal the true authorships of works published anonymously or pseudonymously may be very valuable in solving scholarly problems.[1] A selection of those for some prominent literatures is given in the following paragraphs.

English and American dictionaries of anonyms and pseudonyms include two by William Cushing. These are *Anonyms; A Dictionary of Revealed Authorship* (London and Cambridge, Mass.: Cushing, 1899) and *Initials and Pseudonyms; A Dictionary of Literary Disguises* (2 vols.; New York: Crowell, [1885-88]). To these must be added Samuel Halkett and John Laing, *A Dictionary of Anonymous and Pseudonymous English Literature,* new and enlarged edition by James Kennedy, W. A. Smith, and A. F. Johnson (9 vols.; Edinburgh and London: Oliver & Boyd, 1926-[62]). The ninth volume brings coverage down to 1961 and supplies addenda.

There exist three French counterparts to the above. These are Joseph M. Quérard, *Les Supercheries littéraires dévoilées* (3 vols., 2. éd.; Paris: Féchoz et Letouzey, 1882), Antoine A. Barbier, *Dictionnaire des ouvrages anonymes* (4 vols., 3. éd.; Paris: Daffis, 1872-79), and Gustave Brunet, *Dictionnaire des ouvrages anonymes suivi des Supercheries littéraires dévoilées; Supplément à la dernière édition de ces deux ouvrages* (Paris: Fechoz, 1889). German complements to the Cushing works are those by Michael Holzmann, *Deutsches Anonymenlexikon* (7 vols.; Weimar: Gesellschaft der Bibliophilen), with Hanns Bohatta, and *Deutsches Pseudonymen-Lexikon* (Wien: Akademischer Verlag, 1906).

For Italy one may consult the work by Gaetano Melzi, *Dizionario di opere anonime é pseudonime di scrittori italiani, o come che sia aventi relazione all' Italia* (3 vols.; Milano: Coi Torchi di L. Giacomo Pirola, 1849-59). Supplements were issued in 1887 and 1888 by G. B. Passano and Emmanuele Rocco, respectively. Spanish literature published pseudonymously is unlocked by Eugenio Hartzenbusch e Hiriart, *Unos cuantos seudónimos di escritores españoles con sus correspondientes nombres verdaderos* (Madrid: Rivadeneyra, 1904) and Eduardo Ponce de León Freyre, *1,500 seudónimos modernos de la literatura española (1900-1942)* (Madrid: Instituto Nacional del Libro Español, 1942).

---

[1] For a consideration of such problems in music see Charles L. Cudworth, "Ye Olde Spuriosity Shoppe; Or, Put It in the *Anhang,*" *Music Library Association Notes* XII (1954-55), 25-40 and 533-53.

# CHAPTER VII / Bibliographies

## Subject Bibliographies

For guides to subject bibliographies the reader will want to refer to those works brought out in Chapter II. Especially helpful is the section on "Subject Bibliographies" in Robert L. Collison's *Bibliographies, Subject and National.* Robert B. Downs's and Frances B. Jenkins' *Bibliography; Current State and Future Trends* (Urbana: University of Illinois Press, 1967) contains a study of the music situation by Vincent Duckles entitled "Music Literature, Music, and Sound Recordings." The *Subject Index of Books Published Before 1880* (4 vols.; London: Grafton, 1933-43), by Robert A. Peddie, reflects a vast amount of older literature, but is superseded by the subject catalogues of certain large libraries, which will be brought out in Chapter IX.

W. A. Hammond's *A Bibliography of Aesthetics and of the Philosophy of the Fine Arts from 1900 to 1932* (rev. and enlarged ed.; New York: Longmans, 1934) devotes fifteen pages to a music section compiled with the aid of Oliver Strunk. A recent addition to the scene of the bibliography of the fine arts is the German *Literature, Music, Fine Arts; A Review of German-Language Research Contributions on Literature, Music, and Fine Arts* (Tübingen: [no publisher given], 1968-). This forms section 3 of *German Studies* and is published twice a year. Articles are included and roughly four times as many items are listed as are reviewed.

Paul D. Magriel's *A Bibliography of Dancing; A List of Books and Articles on the Dance and Related Subjects* (with 4 supplements; New York: Wilson, 1936-41) includes references to music and locates copies. The supplements are cumulative. In view of the growing importance of the iconography of music, the scholar will want to take note of Mary W. Chamberlin's *Guide to Art Reference Books* (Chicago: American Library Association, 1959).

The *Theological Book List* by Raymond P. Morris (Oxford: Blackwell, 1960) contains a large number of titles treating Christianity as well as other faiths. Because of its serial nature the literature on religion is kept under control by the annual *International Bibliography of the History of Religions* (Leiden: Brill, 1952-). The organization of this bibliography is principally by religions.

An older, but still valuable work is Benjamin Rand's *Bibliography of Philosophy, Psychology, and Cognate Subjects* (New York: Macmillan, 1905). Philosophy and psychology are each served by a serial bibliography. The first of these is the *Bibliographie de la philosophie* [1937-] (Paris: Vrin, 1938-), in which music is found under section 4 (Philosophy of Art. Aesthetics), while the latter is the *Psychological Abstracts* (Lancaster, Pa.: American Psychological Association, 1927-), whose index reflects "Music."

D. J. Foskett's *How to Find Out; Educational Research* (Oxford: Pergamon, 1936) and the *International Guide to Educational Documentation* (Paris: UNESCO, 1963) should be used in conjunction with the *Education Index* (cf. Chapter VIII). Peter R. Lewis' *The Literature of the Social Sciences; An Introductory Survey and Guide* (London: Library Association, 1960) reflects the literature of the nineteenth and twentieth centuries. Thomas P. Fleming's *Guide to the Literature of Science* (2nd ed.; New York: Columbia University, 1957) affords an introduction to the bibliography of science which may be of service.

In the area of history first mention should be given to the important *Guide to Historical Literature* (cf. Chapter I). Music is only sparsely covered in John Roach's *A Bibliography of Modern History* (Cambridge: University Press, 1968). Eric H. Boehm and Lalit Adolphus have compiled *Historical Periodicals; An Annotated World List of Historical and Related Serial Publications* (Santa Barbara, California and Munich, Germany: Clio Press, 1961), which is organized by country and which has an index of periodicals. Two serial bibliographies are the *Annual Bulletin of Historical Literature* (London: Historical Association, 1911) and the *International Bibliography of Historical Sciences* [1926-] (Paris: Colon, 1930-), the latter containing a valuable geographical index.

A relatively large literature has grown up around medieval studies in recent years, but two older handbooks should be mentioned. A bibliography of historiography for the years 375-1500 is August Potthast's *Bibliotheca historica medii aevi* (2 vols., 2. Auflage; Berlin: Weber, 1896). The first major part of this title, dealing with collections, is being reissued, with additions, as *Repertorium fontium historiae medii aevi, primum ab Augusto Potthast digestum* (Roma: Istituto Storico Italiano per il Medio Aevi, 1962-). Louis J. Paetow's *Guide to the Study of Medieval History* (rev. ed.; New York: Crofts, 1931) includes collections and a section on medieval culture. Next in point of time is John H. Fisher's *The Medieval Literature of Western Europe; A Review of Research, Mainly 1930-1960* (New York: Modern Language Association, 1966), which provides evaluations which may prove especially helpful. Music appears to be well represented in the *International Medieval Bibliography* [1967-] (Minneapolis: Department of History, University of Minnesota, [1968-]), for which a separate subject guide is published. The *Progress of Medieval and*

*Renaissance Studies in the United States and Canada* (25 vols.; Boulder:
University of Colorado, 1923-60) will be very useful for the years covered.
Richard H. Rouse's *Serial Bibliographies for Medieval Studies* (Berkeley and
Los Angeles: University of California Press, 1969) lists three items for music.
   The General Reference and Subject Bibliography Division of the Library of
Congress has published *A Guide to the Study of the United States of America;
Representative Books Reflecting the Development of American Life and Thought*
(Washington: [Government Printing Office], 1960), prepared by Roy F. Basler,
Donald H. Mugridge, and Blanche P. McCrum. Approximately fifty-five pages
are devoted to music. Two large bibliographies of the Soviet Union have been
edited by Paul L. Horecky. The first of these, *Basic Russian Publications; An
Annotated Bibliography on Russia and the Soviet Union* (Chicago: University
of Chicago Press, 1962), contains sections on music by Miloš Velimirović and
Stanley D. Krebs, while for the second, *Russia and the Soviet Union; A
Bibliographic Guide to Western-Language Publications* (Chicago: University
of Chicago Press, 1965), Boris Schwarz has contributed the section on music.
   In the area of linguistics and literatures the Modern Language Association of
America has published the *MLA International Bibliography* as a supplement
to its *Publications* since volume 72 (1957) as well as *A Bibliography on the
Relations of Literature and the Other Arts, 1952-1967* (New York: AMS Press,
1968). Literature is also covered in the "Annual Bibliography" which has been
published as part of the *Yearbook of Comparative and General Literature* since
its volume 1 (1952). For classical languages the basic bibliography is John A.
Nairn's *Classical Hand-List* (4th ed.; Oxford: Blackwell, 1960), which covers
music, but further serial coverage may be gained through *L'année philologique;
Bibliographie critique et analytique de l'antiquité greco-latine* [1924/26-]
(Paris: Société d'Édition "Les Belles Lettres," 1928-). Here music is found
under II C ("Linguistique et philologie; Chant, musique, chorégraphie").
   The *Cambridge Bibliography of English Literature* (4 vols. and supplement;
Cambridge: Cambridge University Press, 1941-57), edited by Frederick W.
Bateson, may be supplemented by the *New Cambridge Bibliography of English
Literature* (Cambridge: University Press, 1969-) and the *Annual Bibliography of
English Language and Literature* [1920-] (Cambridge: University Press, 1921-),
which provides an author and subject index. Jacob Blanck's *Bibliography of
American Literature* (New Haven: Yale University Press, 1955-) provides very
detailed bibliographical descriptions of the literature itself, but no criticism.
Sheet music is entered as found, but was not especially sought for.
   D. C. Cabeen is the general editor of *A Critical Bibliography of French
Literature* ([Syracuse, N.Y.]: Syracuse University Press, 1947-), in which the
order of the volumes is by chronology, but in which the internal arrangement
is by types of material. For example, Guillaume de Machaut is found in the
medieval volume under "Lyric Verse of the Twelfth, Thirteenth, and Fourteenth

Centuries." Continuous coverage in this discipline is afforded through Otto
Kapp's *Bibliographie der französischen Literaturwissenschaft* [1956-]
(Frankfurt am Main: Klostermann, [1960]), in which the internal arrangement
is chronological and which boasts an "Index nominum" and an "Index rerum"
of sizeable proportions. Josef Körner's *Bibliographisches Handbuch des
deutschen Schrifttums* (3. Aufl.; Bern: Francke, 1949) contains German
literature and criticism in a chronological arrangement, with a good index.
For subsequent materials the *Bibliographie der deutschen Literaturwissenschaft*
[1945/53-] (Frankfurt am Main: Klostermann, 1957-) should be consulted.
Guido Mazzoni's *Avviamento allo studio critico delle lettere italiane* (4. ed.;
Firenze: Sansoni, [1951]) follows a systematic arrangement, providing a table
of contents, but no index. Raymond L. Grismer's *New Bibliography of the
Literatures of Spain and Spanish America* (Minneapolis: Perine Book Co., 1941-)
is in alphabetical order, with the keys to abbreviations in the back of the volumes.

In the *International Folklore Bibliography* [1917-] (Basle: Krebs, 1919-),
which is sponsored by the Société Suisse des Traditions Populaires, music will
be found under section 17 ("Music and Dance; Yodler, Yuchzer, etc."). The
*Bibliography of North American Folklore and Folksong* (2 vols., 2nd ed.;
New York: Dover, 1961) includes lists of music and recordings.

In recent years the application of the computer to our discipline has
become important and widespread. Alan Pritchard's *A Guide to Computer
Literature* (Hamden, Conn.: Archon, 1969) handles the literature in a general
way, without providing a subject index. An excellent medium by which one
may keep up with this fast moving field is the periodical *Computers and the
Humanities* (Flushing, N.Y.: Queens College, 1966-). This includes bibliographies,
abstracts, and reviews, and volume 4 contains a special section on "Musicology
and Computers."

## Special Bibliographies

The above section was devoted to those bibliographies which are pointed toward
a special discipline. We now come to book lists which are distinguished by the
physical state of the material, such as periodicals or newspapers, or by the nature
of the literature, such as plays or translations. For the most part the same guides
can be used as were described in the first paragraph under "Subject Bibliographies."

*Ulrich's International Periodicals Directory* (New York: Bowker, [1932-]),
edited by Eileen C. Graves, enjoys a venerable publishing history. The thirteenth
edition (1969-70) reflects thirty-three columns of music periodicals. For
retrospective bibliographical control of periodicals the reader may wish to

consult the *Catalogue of Printed Books; Periodical Publications* (2 vols., 2nd ed.; London: Museum, 1899-1900), of the British Museum Department of Printed Books, or the *Verzeichnis ausgewählter Wissenschaftlicher Zeitschriften des Auslandes VAZ* (with a separate register; Wiesbaden: Steiner, 1957), published by the Deutsche Forschungsgemeinschaft. The register is the title index, but alphabetization is by the key words of the title. Music is found under 9,2 ("Musikwissenschaft"). In the *National Directory of Newsletters and Reporting Services* (Detroit: Gale, 1966) music is found in section 6 ("Humanities"). The publication offers notes on the contents of newsletters, as well as addresses, editors' names, and similar information. The biennial *Irregular Serials and Annuals* (New York: Bowker, 1967-) devotes about seven columns to music, and while not essentially a bibliography, does provide information about price and publisher, as well as other relevant data. A publication, although now somewhat old, which supplies abbreviations conventionally used for many periodical publications is Werner Rust's *Verzeichnis von unklaren Titelkürzungen deutscher und ausländischer Zeitschriften* (Leipzig: Harrassowitz, 1927).

Willing's is an important name in the annals of newspaper guides. The older *Willing's Press Guide* (London: Willing's Press Service, 1874-) services mainly the United Kingdom, with some "Foreign" listings. The listing is by country, with no subject approach. The *Willing's European Press Guide* [1966/67-] (London: Willing, 1966-) lists journals published on the continent and has both a subject approach and an alphabetical index.

Knowledge of the existence of translations of vital material can be extremely time-saving to the scholar. A general ongoing guide to such translations is the *Index translationum; International Bibliography of Translations* (Paris: [various publishers], 1932-). The listing is by country and then by discipline, in which music is found under rubric 7 ("Jeux, Sports"). There is an index of authors at the close of the volumes. Two volumes of *The Literatures of the World in English Translation; A Bibliography* (New York: Ungar, [1967-]) have seen publication. The first of these is *The Greek and Latin Literatures*, compiled by George B. Parks and Ruth Z. Temple, which lists translations through modern Greek and Neo-Latin literature from 1450 A.D. The second volume is *The Slavic Literatures*, by Richard C. Lewanski. The latter volume provides indexes of authors, anthologies, and compilers, as well as individual titles, but the general orientation of the volume is by literatures.

The classical languages are serviced by three individual volumes. These are *English Translations from the Greek; A Bibliographical Survey* (New York: Columbia University Press, 1918), by Finley M. K. Foster, Henrietta R. Palmer's *Lists of English Editions and Translations of Greek and Latin Classics Printed Before 1641* (London: Bibliographical Society, 1911), and *The Classics in Translation; An Annotated Guide to the Best Translations of the Greek and Latin Classics into English* (London: Scribner's, 1930), by Frank Seymour Smith.

The last-named book goes through the eighteenth century. Bayard Q. Morgan's
*A Critical Bibliography of German Literature in English Translation, 1481-1927,
with Supplement Embracing the Years 1928-1935* (2nd ed.; Stanford, Calif.:
Stanford, University Press, 1938) supplies an index of translators and gives some
opera text translations. *English Translations from the Spanish, 1484-1943; A
Bibliography* (New Brunswick, N.J.: Rutgers University Press, 1944), by
Remigio U. Pane, in which the original authors is the method of entry, is
equipped with an index of translators, but no subject index. Of interest to
medievalists is the *Bibliography of English Translations from Medieval Sources*
(New York: Columbia University Press, 1946), by Clarissa P. Farrar and Austin
P. Evans. This annotated volume draws from the fourth to the end of the
fifteenth century.

A comprehensive guide to plays is furnished through Joseph Gregor's *Der
Schauspielführer* (8 vols.; Stuttgart: Hiersemann, 1953-67). Coverage is from
the Middle Ages to 1965. Plot sketches are furnished, and there are various
valuable indexes. H. J. Eldredge's *"The Stage" Cyclopaedia* (London: "The
Stage," 1909), published under the pseudonym Reginald Clarence, provides a
bibliography of nearly fifty thousand plays recorded from the beginning of the
English stage, together with descriptions, authors' names, dates, places of
production, and like items of information. The entries are coded for music,
musical comedy, musical drama, and similar types of treatment. Carl Joseph
Stratman has contributed greatly to the bibliography of the dramatic arts. His
*Bibliography of Medieval Drama* (2 vols., 2nd ed.; New York: Ungar, 1972)
lists editions and studies of the dramas. Proceeding to bibliographies of works
about dramas we should mention Blanche M. Baker's *Theater and Allied Arts;
A Guide to Books Dealing with the History, Criticism, and Technic of the Drama
and Theatre and Related Arts and Crafts* (New York: Blom, 1952) and *Dramatic
Bibliography; An Annotated List of Books on the History and Criticism of the
Drama and Stage and on the Allied Arts of the Theatre* (New York: Blom, 1968),
both of which devote sections to music. Two further titles in this area are Oscar
G. Brockett, Samuel L. Becker, and Donald C. Bryant, *A Bibliographical Guide
to Research in Speech and Dramatic Art* (Glenview, Ill.: Scott, Foresman, [1963])
and David Cheshire, *Theatre; History, Criticism, and Reference* ([Hamden, Conn.]:
Archon, [1967]), the former having a valuable section on "Related Areas."

Because of the presence of music in many incunabula, the scholar should have
access to bibliographies of this material. The basic set is Ludwig Friedrich
Theodor Hain's *Repertorium bibliographicum, in quo libri omnes ab arte
typographica inventa usque ad annum MD* (2 vols.; Stuttgart: Cotta, 1826-38).
The supplements to this are W. A. Copinger, *Supplement to Hain's Repertorium
bibliographicum* (2 vols.; London: Sotheran, 1895-1902), Dietrich Reichling,
*Appendices ad Hainii-Copingeri Repertorivm bibliographicvm* (7 vols; Monachii:
Rosenthal, 1905-11), and Konrad Burger, *Supplement zu Hain und Panzer*

(Leipzig: Hiersemann, 1908). The monumental bibliography, unfortunately incomplete, is the *Gesamtkatalog der Wiegendrucke* [A-Federicis] (7 vols., plus part one of an eighth volume; Leipzig: Hiersemann, 1925-40). Very full information is provided, including location of copies in cases in which ten or less of a single title are known to exist.[1] American locations are given in Frederick R. Goff's *Incunabula in American Libraries; A Third Census of Fifteenth Century Books Recorded in North American Collections* (New York: Bibliographical Society of America, 1964). Edward C. Bigmore and C. W. H. Wyman's *A Bibliography of Printing* (2nd ed.; New York: Duschnes, 1945) provides a list of works on the subject by author or title. There is no subject index.

Eleanora A. Baer's *Titles in Series; A Handbook for Librarians and Students* (2 vols. and supplements, 2nd ed.; New York: Scarecrow, 1964-67) identifies about forty thousand book titles.[2] The series are given in volume 1, with the indexes in volume 2, including a directory of publishers. The supplement adds a large number of titles. A catalogue of series which were never completed is provided by Michael O. Krieg, *Mehr nicht erschienen; Ein Verzeichnis unvollendet gebliebener Druckwerke* (2 vols.; Bad Bocklet: Krieg, 1954-58). Dobell Bertram's *Catalogue of Books Printed for Private Circulation* (London: [The Author], 1906) provides entry by author or title, with no subject index. The reader should not overlook the small "Second Alphabet" at the end of the volume.

Bibliographical control for a segment of German autobiographical literature is furnished by Ingrid Bode's *Die Autobiographien zur deutschen Literatur, Kunst und Musik, 1900-1965* (Stuttgart: Metzlersche Verlagsbuchhandlung, [1966]). While there is no subject index which reflects music, there is a large index of persons represented in individual works. German scholarly pamphlets known as "Programmschriften," which were widely published and exchanged in the period before World War I, may be of very great importance to the scholar. A classified comprehensive catalogue of this material is provided through Rudolf Klussmann's *Systematisches Verzeichnis der Abhandlungen welche in den Schulschriften sämtlicher an den Programmtausche teilnehmenden Lehranstalten erschienen sind* [1876-1910] (5 vols; Leipzig: Teubner, 1889-1916).[3]

---

[1] Kathi Meyer-Baer's *Liturgical Music Incunabula; A Descriptive Catalog* (London: The Bibliographical Society, 1962) is a bibliography directed expressly toward music. Locations are provided.

[2] A bibliography for music literature with similar intent is Fred Blum's *Music Monographs in Series; A Bibliography of Numbered Monograph Series in the Field of Music Since 1945* (New York: Scarecrow Press, 1964).

[3] The accessibility of such material to the American scholar is greatly enhanced by the presence of the collection represented in the *Catalog of the Programmschriften Collection; The University of Pennsylvania Library* (Boston: Hall, 1961). The catalogue represents the humanities section, or about one-third of the collection of 16,555 pamphlets.

## Bibliographies of Theses and Dissertations

In a manner of speaking, bibliographies of theses and dissertations are special bibliographies. They form such a unique and viable group by themselves, however, that it is well to treat them in a separate section.

In the area of bibliographies of bibliographies of dissertations two works may be cited. The first of these is the American *Guide to Bibliographies of Theses, United States and Canada* (2nd ed.; Chicago: American Library Association, 1940), by Thomas R. Palfrey and Henry E. Coleman, Jr. Although perhaps not primarily intended as such, a publication which may serve in this same way for Great Britain is Peter D. Record's *A Survey of Thesis Literature in British Libraries* (London: The Library Association, 1950).

The following survey is limited to either national listings or listings devoted to more than one university. Because of limitations of space neither individual library holdings nor individual abstract series can be taken into account.

Proceeding to dissertation bibliographies, the *List of American Doctoral Dissertations* [1912-38] (26 vols.; Washington: Government Printing Office, 1913-40), published by the Catalog Division of the Library of Congress, includes a subject index. The *Doctoral Dissertations Accepted by American Universities* [1933/34-1954/55] (New York: Wilson, 1934-56), in which an alphabetical subject index was published, has been superseded by the monumental *Dissertation Abstracts International; Abstracts of Dissertations Available on Microfilm or as Xerographic Reproductions* (Ann Arbor: University Microfilms, 1938-). To 1951 the title of the series was *Microfilm Abstracts,* while from that year to 1969 the title was *Dissertation Abstracts.* The new title reflects the international character of the publication, particularly the inclusion of dissertations from Europe. From volume 16 (1955-56) on, number 13 of the annual volume was entitled "Index to American Doctoral Dissertations." Canadian dissertations were included. Beginning with the 1964-65 issue this is being published separately under the title *American Doctoral Dissertations,* a publication listing all dissertations accepted by American and Canadian universities, not only those included in *Dissertation Abstracts International.* The former includes an informative section on "Publication, Preservation and Lending of American Doctoral Dissertations." The index reflects "Music," with no breakdown. *Dissertation Abstracts International* itself contains abstracts sent in by cooperating institutions together with the prices of microfilms and xerographic prints of the dissertations themselves. Beginning with volume 22 (1961-62) a detailed subject index was included in each number. From volume 27 (1966-67) on, the large series has been appearing in two subseries, A (The Social Sciences and Humanities) and B (The Physical Sciences and Engineering). Each subseries is paginated separately. Keyword title and author indexes are published each month and are cumulated separately at the end of the year for each section. From volume 30 (1969-70) on, a mechanized keyword title index classifies and arranges the bibliographic entries. Each issue of Sections A and B provides this and an author index, and each of the indexes is cumulated annually. The cumulated subject and author indexes to volume 29 (1968-69) show a great many subdivisions under "Music." An index for the years 1938 to 1968-69 has been published under the title *Dissertation Abstracts International; Retrospective Index, Volumes I-XXIX* (8 vols.; [no place] : Xerox, 1970), of which volume 8 is devoted to Communication Information / Business / Literature / Fine Arts.

Bibliographical control of master's theses is provided through Dorothy M. Black's *Guide to Lists of Master's Theses* (Chicago: American Library Association, 1965). This is essentially a bibliography of bibliographies in which music is reflected in part 3, "Lists of Master's Theses in Special Fields." A publication which to some extent parallels *Dissertation Abstracts International,* but on the master's level, is *Masters Abstracts; Abstracts of Selected Masters Theses on Microfilm* (Ann Arbor: University Microfilms, 1962-). A subject arrangement is used, with a limited number of theses in music being represented.

The annual *Canadian Theses; Thèses canadiennes* [1960/61] (Ottawa: National Library of Canada, 1962-) provides a subject and an author index, the former simply listing "Music—Musique." Retrospective Canadian coverage is afforded through the *Canadian Graduate Theses in the Humanities and Social Sciences, 1921-1946* (Ottawa: Printer to the King, 1951). This publication provides brief indications of the contents of the theses. The Public Archives of Canada have sponsored the *Register of Post-Graduate Dissertations in Progress in History and Related Subjects* ([Ottawa] : Canadian Historical Association, [1966-]) which also provides information about foreign theses having to do with Canadian topics.

Austrian dissertations submitted from the year 1966 on are listed in the *Gesamtverzeichnis österreichischer Dissertationen* (Wien: Verlag Notring der wissenschaftlichen Verbände Österreichs, 1967-). This publication is organized by university, then by faculty. Earlier coverage for the Universities of Vienna and (in part) Innsbruck is to be found in the *Verzeichnis über die seit dem Jahre 1872 an der philosophischen Fakultät der Universität in Wien eingereichten und approbierten Dissertationen* (7 vols.; Wien: [various publishers], 1935-59) in the limited way suggested by the title. In volume 4 the coverage was made retrospective for Innsbruck University, and both universities were continued together to 1937. The coverage of the set, the title of which varies, extends to 1957. Dissertations are also included in the *Österreichische Bibliographie* (cf. Chapter III).

France has coverage from 1884/85 by way of the *Catalogue des thèses et écrits académiques* (Paris: [various publishers], 1885-), published by the Ministère de l'Education Nationale. Retrospective survey is afforded through two works by Albert Maire, *Catalogue des thèses des sciences soutenues en France de 1810 à 1890* (Paris: Welter, 1892) and *Répertoire alphabétique des thèses de doctorat ès lettres des universités françaises, 1810-1900* (Paris: Picard, 1903). The work by

Athénaïs Mourier and F. Deltour, *Notice sur le doctorat ès lettres, suivie du catalogue et de l'analyse des thèses françaises et latines admises par les facultés des lettres depuis 1810* (4. éd.; Paris: Delalain, 1880), has been supplemented by the *Catalogue et analyse des thèses latines et françaises* (21 vols.; 1882-1901). The *Bibliographie de la France* (cf. Chapter III) has lists of theses beginning with the year 1930. They are presently found in Supplement D.

Two basic German series may be cited. The first of these is the *Jahresverzeichnis der deutschen Hochschulschriften* [1885-] (Berlin and Leipzig: [various publishers], 1887-). The internal organization of the set varies. The second series is the *Bibliographischer Monatsbericht über neu erschienene Schul-, Universitäts- und Hochschulschriften* [1889/90-1942/43] (54 vols.; Leipzig: Fock, 1890-1943). Retrospective coverage may be found in the work by Hermann Mundt, *Bio-bibliographisches Verzeichnis von Universitäts- u. Hochschuldrucken (Dissertationen) vom Ausgang des 16. bis Ende des 19. Jahrhunderts* (incomplete, includes A-Ritter; Leipzig: Carlsohn, 1936-). Swiss dissertations are under excellent bibliographical control through the *Jahresverzeichnis der schweizerischen Hochschulschriften / Catalogue des écrits académiques suisses* [1897-] (Basel: [various publishers], 1898-).

For Great Britain the important bibliography for recent years is the *Index to Theses Accepted for Higher Degrees in the Universities of Great Britain and Ireland* [1950/51-] (London: Aslib, 1953-). Of particular interest to the musicologist may be the *Historical Research for University Degrees in the United Kingdom* [1931/32-] (London: Longmans, 1933-), published by the Institute of Historical Research in London.

Current Netherlandic dissertations are listed in the *Catalogus van academische Geschriften in Nederland verschenen* [1924-] ([place varies]: Nederlandsche Vereeniging van Bibliothecarissen, 1925-). For earlier coverage one should consult J. W. Wijndelts' *Catalogus van academische Proefschriften, verdedigd aan de Nederlandsche Universiteiten gedurende de Jaren 1815-1900* (2 vols.; Groningen: Evers, 1901-3). This publication includes Leyden, Utrecht, Groningen, and Amsterdam Universities.

Scandinavian and Finnish dissertation bibliographies must be considered as a group, since there is considerable overlapping. In roughly chronological order they are as follows: Johan Henrik Liden, *Catalogus disputationum in academiis et gymnasiis Sueciae atque etiam a Suecis extra patriam habitarum, quotquot huc usque reperii potuerunt* (5 parts; Upsaliae: Typ. Erdmannianis, 1778-80); Gabriel Marklin, *Catalogus disputationum in academiis Scandinaviae et Finlandiae* [1778-1819] (3 parts, with a supplement of 1820; Upsaliae: Reg. Academiae Typ., 1820) and *Catalogus disputationum in academiis Sveciae et Fenniae habitarum* [1820-55] (3 parts; Upsala: Vahlström, 1856); Aksel G. S. Josephson, *Avhandlingar ock program, uitg. vid svenska ock finska ock skolor, 1855-1890* (2 vols.; Uppsala: I kommission hos Lundequistska Bokhandeln [1891-97]);

Samuel Erik Melander, *Förteckning öfver afhandlingar och uppsatser som ingå i eller medfölja årsredogörelserna för rikets allmänna läroverk, 1858-1909* (2 vols.; Lund: Ohlsson, 1909-12); Axel Herman Nelson, *Akademiska afhandlingar vid Sveriges universitet och högskolor läsåren 1890/91-1909/10 jämte förteckning öfver svenskars akademiska afhandlingar vid utländska universitet under samma tid* (Uppsala: Akademiska Bokhandeln, [1911-12]); and John Tuneld, *Akademiska avhandlingar vid sveriges universitet ock hogskolor, läsåren 1910/11-1939/40; Bibliografi* (Lund: [Ohlsson], 1945), which enters six items under "Musik och teater." To this list may be added *Danish Theses for the Doctorate and Commemorative Publications of the University of Copenhagen, 1836-1926; A Bio-bibliography* (Copenhagen: Levin & Munksgaard, 1929) and *Danish Theses for the Doctorate, 1927-1958; A Bibliography* (Copenhagen: University Library, 1962), which enters seven theses under "Music."

# CHAPTER VIII / Indexes and Directories

A VERY USEFUL bibliographical key to indexes is Norma O. Ireland's *An Index to Indexes* (Boston: Faxon, 1942). General information about indexing is provided in Robert L. Collison's *Indexes and Indexing* (cf. Chapter I).

## General Literary Indexes

A general index is the American Library Association's *Index to General Literature* (2nd ed.; Boston and New York: Houghton, Mifflin, 1901). A supplement covering the years 1900-1910 was published in 1914. Its continuation is the *Essay and General Literature Index, 1900-1933* (New York: Wilson, 1934), which devotes fifteen columns to references on music. Supplements exist for 1934-40, 1941-47, 1948-54, 1955-59, 1960-64, 1965, 1966, and 1967. The analysis appears to be limited to English-language publications.

Special indexes include Mary H. Eastman, *Index to Fairy Tales, Myths and Legends* (2nd rev. and enlarged ed.; Boston: Faxon, 1926), to which a supplement was published in 1937, and Dorothy E. Cook and Isabel S. Monro, *Short Story Index* (plus supplements; New York: Wilson, 1953). Wilhelm Olbrich's *Der Romanführer* (15 vols.; Stuttgart: Hiersemann, 1950-71) gives the contents of novels of world literature.

Edith Granger's *Index to Poetry* (5th ed.; New York: Columbia University Press, 1962) indexes anthologies published through 1965 with the aid of its supplement (1965). The *Motif of Folk-Literature* (6 vols., rev. and enlarged ed.; Bloomington: Indiana University Press, 1955-58), by Stith Thompson, contains a "General Synopsis of the Index" in volume 1, with detailed synopses provided in each volume. Beyond this, there is a general index in the final volume. Further indexes to poetry are the *Subject Index to Poetry* (Chicago: American Library Association, 1940), by H. Bruncken, or Edith Granger's *Index to Poetry and Recitations* (5th ed.; New York: Columbia University Press, 1962), with a supplement of 1967. The latter work is organized by title and first line index, with author and subject indexes.

Numerous play indexes have been published. In approximately chronological order these are Hannah Logasa and Winifred Ver Nooy, *Index to One-Act Plays* [1900-] (5 vols.; Boston: Faxon, 1924-58); Ina Ten Eyck Firkins, *Index to Plays, 1800-1926* (New York: Wilson, 1927), with a supplement for 1927-34 (1935); Dorothy H. West, Estelle A. Fidell, and Dorothy M. Peake, *Play Index, 1949-1952* (New York: Wilson, 1953), with supplements for 1953-60 (1963) and 1961-67 (1968); and John H. Ottemiller, *Index to Plays in Collections . . . Published Between 1900 and 1962* (4th ed.; New York: Scarecrow, 1964).

## Periodical and Newspaper Indexes

As a guide to this type of material, one may wish to consult Daniel C. Haskell, *A Check List of Cumulative Indexes to Individual Periodicals in the New York Public Library* (New York: New York Public Library, 1962) or Jean S. Kujoth, *Subject Guide to Periodical Indexes and Review Indexes* (Metuchen, N.J.: Scarecrow Press, 1969). The latter presents thirteen titles relating to music, with further references.

There exist two periodical indexes of international coverage. The first of these is Abteilung B of the *Internationale Bibliographie der Zeitschriftenliteratur,* entitled *Bibliographie der fremdsprachigen Zeitschriftenliteratur* (71 vols.; [place varies]: Dietrich, 1911-64). From the issue for 1965 this has been appearing under the first-named title in a "Kombinierte Folge." There are three basic parts: A, index of periodicals consulted; B, classified subject index of articles published; and C, index of authors. The first half-volume for 1968 shows sixteen catch-words dealing with music, covering seven columns. The *International Index to Periodicals* [1907-] (New York: Wilson, 1916-) is now entitled *Social Sciences and Humanities Index.* It covers English-language periodicals, appears quarterly, and is cumulated. Nearly two columns were devoted to music in the 1968-69 volume.

Among the American and English indexes *Poole's Index to Periodical Literature, 1802-1881* (rev. ed.; Boston: Houghton, Mifflin, 1891) has issued supplements for 1882-86, 1887-91, 1892-96, 1897-1901, and 1902-6. A cumulative author index exists for 1802-1906 (Ann Arbor: Pierian Press, 1971). For the period 1890-1922 one may consult the *Nineteenth Century Readers' Guide to Periodical Literature* (2 vols.; New York: Wilson, 1944). The *Readers' Guide to Periodical Literature* (New York: Wilson, 1905-) began its indexing with the year 1900. In 1947-49, just prior to the inception of the *Music Index,* music periodicals analyzed were *Musical America,* the *Musical Quarterly,* and the *Musician.* The *Annual Magazine Subject Index* [1907-49] (Boston: [various publishers], 1908-52), which absorbed the *Magazine Subject Index* [1907] (Boston: Boston Book Co., 1908) in 1909, is particularly good for local history. It has recently been republished as the *Cumulated Magazine Subject Index, 1907-1949; A Cumulation of the F. W. Faxon Company's Annual Magazine Subject Index* (2 vols.; Boston: Hall, 1964), where twenty-three columns are devoted to music.

The British *Subject Index to Periodicals* [1915-61] (47 vols.; London: [various publishers], 1919-62) indexed the *Musical Times*. Its successor, the *British Humanities Index* [1962-] (London: The Library Association, 1963-) provides author and subject sections and in its 1968 volume indexed fifteen music journals. Wales is represented through the *Subject Index to Welsh Periodicals* [1931-] (Swansea: The Library Association, 1934-). The *Canadian Periodical Index* (Ottawa: Canadian Library Association, 1964-) is a continuation of the *Canadian Index* (1948-50) and the *Canadian Index to Periodicals and Documentary Films* (1951-63), and in its 1968 volume provided the headings "music," "musical," "musicians," and "musicology," and indexed *Arts Canada* and *Performing Arts in Canada*.

Two indexes to "little magazines" are the *Index to Little Magazines* [1943-] (Denver: Swallow, 1949-) and the *Index to Commonwealth Little Magazines* [1964/65-] (New York: Johnson Reprint, 1966-). A retrospective index which will undoubtedly grow in significance as it progresses is the *Wellesley Index to Victorian Periodicals, 1824-1900* ([Toronto]: University of Toronto Press, [1966-]).

Other American indexes of possible aid to the music historian are the *Art Index* [1929-] (New York: Wilson, 1933-); the *Education Index* [1929-] (New York: Wilson, 1932-); the *Film Index* (New York: [various publishers], 1941-); and the *Guide to the Performing Arts* [1957-] (New York: Scarecrow, 1960-), the compiler of the latter being S. Yancey Belknap.

France is singularly lacking in periodical indexes as such, with the exception of the short-lived *Répertoire bibliographique des principales revues françaises* [1897-99] (3 vols.; Paris: Per Lamm, 1898-1901). In view of this dearth, the reader should be aware of three works which analyze the publications of learned societies: Robert Charles Lasteyrie du Saillant, *Bibliographie générale des travaux historiques et archéologiques publiés par les sociétés savantes de la France* (6 vols.; Paris: Imprimerie Nationale, 1888-1918), the *Bibliographie annuelle des travaux historiques et archéologiques publiés par les sociétés savantes de la France* [1901/2-1909/10] (3 vols.; Paris: Imprimerie Nationale, 1906-14), and René Gandilhon, *Bibliographie générale des travaux historiques et archéologiques publiés par les sociétés savantes de la France* [1910-40] (5 vols.; Paris: Imprimerie Nationale, 1944-61). The *Bulletin signalétique* (22 vols.; Paris: Centre de Documentation du Centre Nationale de la Recherche Scientifique, 1947-68) is an abstracting service international in coverage, but leaning toward French publications. The placement of music varies, but is often found within section 19, "Sciences humains, philosophie." The *Bibliographie de Belgique* (cf. Chapter III) covers Belgian periodical literature for the years 1897-1914 and 1921-25.

German periodical literature from 1896 to 1964 is covered in Abteilung A of the *Internationale Bibliographie der Zeitschriftenliteratur,* which is the *Bibliographie der deutschen Zeitschriftenliteratur* (128 vols.; [place varies: various publishers], 1897-1964). For coverage since 1964 one should consult the "Kombinierte Folge" of the former title, discussed earlier in this chapter. Retrospective coverage for 1861-95 (and even later) is provided in the twenty volumes of "Ergänzungsbände."

For the Netherlands one can consult *Nijhoff's Index op de nederlandsche periodieken van algemeenen inhoud* ('s Gravenhage: Nijhoff, 1910-), beginning coverage with the year 1909. Danish periodical literature for 1855-1912 is analyzed in the *Danske blandede tidsskrifter* (2 vols.; København: Bianco Lunos, 1928-29), while the period from 1915 onward is represented in the *Danske tidsskrift-index* (København: [various publishers], 1916-). For Norway one should see the *Norsk tidsskriftindex* [1918-] (Oslo: [various publishers], 1919-), while for Sweden the *Svenska tidskriftsartiklar* (Lund: Bibliotekstjänst, 1952-) is available.

As the title indicates, the Italian *Pubblicazioni edite dallo stato o col suo concorso* [1901-] (Roma: Libreria dello Stato, 1926-) indexes publications published either by the government or with its aid. Despite this, the coverage is rather wide, and a subject approach is used.

In the *Bibliografija jugoslavije; Članci i prilozi u časopisima i listovima* (cf. Chapter III), music is found under "Serija C." The Rumanian *Bibliografia analitică a periodicelor românești* (Bucareşti: Editura Academiei Republicii Socialiste România, 1966-) places music under the rubric "78" and begins its coverage with the year 1790. Hungarian references to music may be located under "780" in the *Magyar folyóiratok repertóriuma; Repertorium bibliographicum periodicorum hungaricorum* (Budapest: Országos Széchényi Könyvtár, 1946-). Music (Hudba) is found under the rubric XXVIII.5.C5 in the Czech *Články v českých časopisech* (V Praze: Národní Knihovna, 1953-).[1]

Bulgarian periodicals are analyzed in the *Letopis na periodichniia pechat* (Sofia: Bulgarski Bibliografski Institut, 1952-), while the Russian periodicals index is the *Letopis' zhurnal'nykh stateĭ* (Moskva: [various publishers], 1926-). In the latter title, music is to be found under XXVIII ("Art").

Newspaper indexes are published for certain countries—for example the *Avis-Kronik-Index* (København: Munksgaard, 1940-) for Denmark or the *Letopis' gazetnykh stateĭ* (Moskva: Vsesoiuznaia Kniznaia Palata, 1936-) for the Soviet Union. For the latter nation, the production is made much more

---

1 The interested reader is directed to Zdenek Vyborny, "Czech Music Literature since World War II," *Music Library Association Notes* XVI (1958-59), 539-46.

accessible to the English reader through the *Current Digest of the Soviet Press* (New York: Joint Committee on Soviet Studies, 1949-), which provides translations of selected articles as well as indexes to leading newspapers. In addition to these, certain large newspapers publish their own indexes. For British materials the useful *Index to the Times* [1906-] (London: The Times, 1907-) gives greater detail than does *Palmer's Index to The Times Newspaper* [1790-1941] (London: Palmer, 1868-1943), although the latter is valuable for its early coverage. The *New York Times Index* (New York: New York Times, 1913-) is supplemented by an index on microfilm which covers the years 1851-58, 1860, and 1863-June 1905. Retrospective indexing is now appearing in a *Prior Series,* beginning coverage with the year 1851. The first volume to be available was *The New York Times Index for the Published News of 1863-1874* (New York: Bowker, [1966]).

Finally, two recent serial indexes are providing valuable keys to material published within proceedings of various kinds. The first of these, in point of time, is *Proceedings in Print* ([Mattapan, Mass.]: Proceedings in Print, 1964-), which is now affording a wide spectrum of subject coverage. The cumulative index to volume 6 includes references to several aspects of music. Series SSH (Social Sciences / Humanities) of the *Directory of Published Proceedings* (White Plains, N.Y.: InterDok, 1968-) lists proceedings of conferences, meetings, seminars, symposia, and congresses. No cumulative index has yet come out, but each quarterly issue has a subject/sponsor index.

## Book Reviews

Richard A. Gray's *A Guide to Book Review Citations; A Bibliography of Sources* ([Columbus]: The Ohio State University Press, 1968) guides the user to indexes and bibliographies of review references. It is in classified order, and music may be found in items 482-486.

Book reviews are provided in Abteilung C of the *Internationale Bibliographie der Zeitschriftenliteratur,* which is entitled *Bibliographie der Rezensionen* [1900-43] (77 vols.; [place varies]: Dietrich, 1901-44). In the United States a major source is the *Book Review Digest* (New York: Wilson, 1905-).

*Books Abroad* (Norman: University of Oklahoma Press, 1927-) is issued quarterly. It uses a classification scheme and includes articles, comments on foreign books, and a periodicals survey. Another quarterly is the *Index to Book Reviews in the Humanities* (Detroit: Phillip Thomson, 1960-). In its volume 3, number 1, it indexed fourteen music journals. A non-serial title pointing towards reviews is James M. Salem's *A Guide to Critical Reviews* (New York: Scarecrow, 1966-). Volume 2 indexes reviews of Broadway musicals. Reviews of non-classical records are included in the "Record and Tape Section" of the *Multi Media Reviews Index* [1970-] (Ann Arbor: Pierian Press, 1971-).

## Directories

The number of directories of various types is legion. Some, because of their bibliographical or other specialized nature, will be found elsewhere in this book. Following is a selection which may be of particular interest to the scholar in music.

Publishers and booksellers are listed by country in the *Publisher's International Year Book; World Directory of Book Publishers* (London: Wales, c1960). The entries are coded for coverage (whereby MUS stands for music publishers), and there is an appendix of "International Booksellers," by country. Mary B. Ross's *Directory of Publishing Opportunities* (2nd ed.; Orange, N.J.: Academic Media, 1973) contains a lengthy section on the humanities. The *AB Bookman's Yearbook* ([Newark, N.J.: Antiquarian Bookman], 1954-) lists book and music dealers in the United States. Its British counterpart is the *Small Booksellers & Collectors Directory* ([2nd ed.] ; Wilbarston [Market Harborough, Leics.] : G. Coe, 1967). The latter contains a large "Supplement of Overseas Booksellers" and a subject index.

The *Minerva; Jahrbuch der gelehrten Welt* ([place varies: various publishers], 1891-) is a venerable directory to institutions of higher learning. The basic listing is by place, with indexing to persons. The *Index generalis; General Yearbook of Universities* (Paris: [various publishers], 1919-) directs the reader to higher educational institutions, academies, archives, libraries, scientific institutes, museums, and similar places. The *World of Learning* (London: Europa, 1947-) is a basic listing by country, with an index of institutions. The *Research Centers Directory* (3rd ed.; Detroit: Gale, 1968) records centers which have been established for particular research purposes, often within universities or colleges, within the United States. Music is placed under the section for the Social Sciences, Humanities, and Religion.

The bibliography of association directories is served by the *Association Index; A Source List of Directories and Other Publications Listing Associations* (Los Angeles: Metropolitan Research Co., 1958). This lists over one thousand directories and is provided with indexes, one of which is a subject index. *The 1,978 International Organizations Founded Since the Congress of Vienna* (Brussels: Union of International Associations, 1957) presents a listing in chronological order of organizations which were established between the years 1815 and 1956. The *Yearbook of International Organizations* (Brussels: Union of International Associations, 1948-) is a biennial publication of which *Who's Who in International Organizations* [1962/63] (Brussels: Union of International Organizations, [no date] ) is an index. Music is to be found under "Arts, Literature, Radio, Cinema, TV." One can ascertain meeting times of international societies through the *World List of Future International Meetings* (Washington: Library of Congress, 1959) or the *International Congress Calendar* [1960/61-] (Brussels: Union of International Associations, 1961-). In the former, humanities are to be found in part 2, while in the latter the index reflects "Music," "Musicians," and "Musicology." The *Encyclopedia of Associations* (3 vols., 6th ed.; Detroit: Gale, [1970]) lists a large number of associations, concentrating on the United States and treating European associations only peripherally. In conjunction with these directories one may wish to use F. A. Buttress' *World List of Abbreviations* (3rd ed.; London: Hill, 1966), which presents abbreviations and their resolutions for associations, societies, committees, and similar groups.

The *Foundation Directory* (3rd ed.; New York: Sage, 1967) is a listing of foundations in the United States, organized by State. The index of fields of interest shows ten such foundations with application to music, but more are given under "Arts." The *Annual Register of Grant Support* (Los Angeles: Academic Media, 1969-) records subject information as well as monetary figures and the extent of the grant. Paul Wasserman's *Awards, Honors, and Prizes; A Directory and Source Book* (Detroit: Gale, 1969) reflects music in the subject index. Leo Pride's *International Theatre Directory; A World Directory of the Theatre and Performing Arts* (New York: Simon and Schuster, 1973) gives addresses, capacities, and information on musical performances.

WHEREAS THE PRECEDING CHAPTERS have treated the searching out of various types of materials by the use of bibliographies, indexes, and similar tools, this chapter will be devoted to the locating of these materials in their physical forms.

Prefatory to an account of individual library catalogues, mention should be made of auction records. These may be the key to the origin and disposal of manuscripts or books which have been sold. American catalogues are *American Book Prices Current; A Record of Literary Properties Sold at Auction in the United States and in London, England* [1894/95-] (New York: [various publishers], 1895-) and the *United States Cumulative Book Auction Records* [1940-] (New York: Want List, 1941-). British sets are *Book Prices Current* [1886-] (London: [various publishers], 1888-) and *Book-Auction Records; A Priced and Annotated Annual Record of London Book-Auctions* [1902-] (London: [various publishers], 1903-). Similar publications exist in other countries of Europe, for example, *La Cote international des livres et manuscrits* [1964/65-] (Paris: Publisol, [no date]), which covers France, Belgium, and Switzerland, and the *Jahrbuch der Auktionspreise für Bücher, Handschriften und Autographen* [1950-] (Hamburg: Hauswedel, [no date]), covering Germany, Holland, Austria, and Switzerland.

## Union Lists

A union list, or union catalogue, reflects the holdings of more than one library. Usually an author catalogue, it may represent all books or a selection of books. If the latter, the limitation is usually by subject or type of material. The number of entries for a given title is often limited to one, with appropriate cross references being kept to a minimum. A survey of world union catalogues is provided in Louise N. Malclès' *Manuel de bibliographie* (Paris: Presses Universitaires de France, 1963), where chapter 6 is entitled "Catalogues collectifs de bibliothèques."

The *Union List of Serials in Libraries of the United States and Canada* (5 vols 3rd ed.; New York: Wilson, 1965) provides excellent bibliographical control for serials as well as locations of such items. Entries are by the latest title of the publication, but cross references are provided for changed titles, which occur frequently in the case of serials with a long publishing history. The music scholar will note that music periodicals and scholarly editions series are represented, but not "complete works" sets. In view of the great expansion of music series in the post-World War II period, the user will want to observe that no serials published initially after 1949 are to be found in the *Union List,* but rather in *New Serial Titles; A Union List of Serials Commencing Publication after December 31, 1949* (Washington: Library of Congress, 1953-). Monthly issues of *New Serial Titles* are superseded by quarterly, annual, quinquennial, decennial and vigentennial cumulations or editions. There is also, published separately and monthly, a classed subject arrangement, but subject approach to the cumulations to 1965 is provided in the *Subject Index to New Serial Titles* (Ann Arbor: Pierian Press, 1968). The Dewey classification number 780 is utilize for music, which is furnished with eleven subheadings. In recent years other count of the world have established serials union lists, most prominent among them bein the *British Union Catalogue of Periodicals; A Record of the Periodicals of the World, from the Seventeenth Century to the Present Day, in British Libraries* (4 vols., with supplement; London: Butterworth, 1955-62) and the *Catalogue collectif des périodiques du début du XVII siècle à 1939 conservés dans les bibliothèques de Paris et dans les bibliothèques universitaires des départements* (Paris: Bibliothèque Nationale, 1967-). The latter emphasizes French periodical.

The *Union List of Microfilms, Cumulation 1949-1959* (2 vols.; Ann Arbor: Edwards, 1961), issued by the Philadelphia Bibliographical Center and Union Library Catalogue, may be of considerable aid to the scholar wishing to locate in the United States a film of a manuscript or of a rare book. The *National Register of Microform Masters* (Washington: Library of Congress, 1955-) gives the locations of films which may be used for copying purposes. This serial is divided into three parts, of which part 2, "Alphabetical List of Microform Masters for Which Card Numbers Have Not Been Located" contains the rare material. Eva M. Tilton's *A Union List of Publications in Opaque Microforms* (2nd ed.; New York: Scarecrow, 1964) provides a union list of the publications of a number of publishers, but does not give locations.

## Library Book Catalogues

The discussion of library catalogues has been divided into two sections—catalogues of printed books and catalogues of manuscripts. Unfortunately, because of space limitations, only nationwide surveys or the catalogues of national libraries and collections can be taken into account here.[1] Because of the relatively high amount of duplication of books from library to library, fewer institutions are delineated in this section than will be in the following section.

In recent years the patron has been presented with a number of library directories international in scope. In the *International Library Directory; A World Directory of Libraries* (3rd ed.; London: Wales, c1968), the subjects of libraries are coded, whereby music is indicated as MUS. Klaus G. Saur's *World Guide to Libraries* (3 vols., 2nd ed.; New York: Bowker, 1968) presents in the index volume a geographical index, subject index (with music, dancing, and theater coded together), an international bibliography of library directories, and a list of addresses of the libraries' associations. Two books by Richard C. Lewanski are more or less companion volumes. These are the *European Library Directory; A Geographical and Bibliographical Guide* (Firenze: Olschki, 1968) and *Subject Collections in European Libraries* (New York: Bowker, 1965). Some seven thousand public, university, and special libraries are provided in the former volume. In either publication music is delineated under the number 780.[2]

Beyond this, a number of guides exists for individual countries, of which some prominent ones may serve as examples. The *Aslib Directory; A Guide to Sources of Information in Great Britain and Ireland* (2 vols., 3rd ed.; London: Aslib, 1958) contains Medicine, the Social Sciences, and the Humanities in its volume 2, with numerous references to music in the subject index. "Musique" is entered in the index in volume 3 of the French *Répertoire des bibliothèques d'étude et organismes de documentation* (3 vols.; Paris: Bibliothèque Nationale, 1963). Volume 3 of the *Annuario delle biblioteche italiane* (3 vols., 2. ed.; Roma: Palombi, [1956]) is of particular significance since it contains Roman and Vatican libraries. In addition to the above, certain institutional directories mentioned in Chapter VIII also contain information about libraries and similar establishments.

Introductory guides to the libraries discussed below are Arundell Esdaille, *National Libraries of the World* (2nd ed.; London: Library Association, 1957), and Margaret Burton, *Famous Libraries of the World* (London: Grafton, 1937). In the former handbook statistics for music are occasionally supplied.

Users of American Libraries can consult the *American Library Directory* (New York: Bowker, 1923-) or Lee Ash and Denis Lorenz, *Subject Collections;*

---

[1] The music collections of European national libraries are surveyed in Keith E. Mixter, "Music in the National Libraries of Europe," *College Music Symposium* VIII (1968), 95-101.

[2] The reader should be aware of the *Directory of Music Research Libraries, Including Contributors to the International Inventory of Musical Sources,* compiled by Rita Benton (preliminary ed.; Iowa City: University of Iowa, 1967-).

*A Guide to Special Book Collections and Subject Emphases as Reported by
. . . Libraries in the United States and Canada* (3rd ed.; New York: Bowker,
1967). Robert B. Downs's *American Library Resources; A Bibliographical
Guide* (with supplements; Chicago: American Library Association, 1951)
cites printed references to American collections, by subject.

The U.S. Library of Congress in Washington has published a distinguished
series of catalogues whose bibliographical value cannot be overestimated.
They are the successors to the older depository card catalogues which were
placed in various libraries throughout the United States.

The first, in point of time, is *A Catalogue of Books Represented by Library
of Congress Printed Cards Issued to July 31, 1942* (167 vols.; Ann Arbor:
Edwards, 1942-46). Its supplement is *Cards Issued August 1, 1942-December
31, 1947* (42 vols.; Ann Arbor: Edwards, 1948). Subsequent to these is the
*Library of Congress Author Catalog . . . 1948-1952* (24 vols.; Ann Arbor:
Edwards, 1953). On January 1, 1956, the Library of Congress Catalog was
expanded into the *National Union Catalog.* As a result of this very significant
change the publication from this point on includes titles with the imprints 1956
or later reported by other North American libraries, with locations, as well as
Library of Congress printed catalogue cards. The first quinquennial edition was
for the period 1953/1957 (28 vols.; Ann Arbor: Edwards, 1958); volume 27 of
this edition is entitled *Music and Phonorecords.* The *National Union Catalog* is
continued by monthly supplements, with quarterly, annual, and quinquennial
cumulations (of which *Music and Phonorecords* forms a separate unit). Quinquennial cumulations to date include those for *1958-1962* (54 vols.; New York:
Rowman & Littlefield, 1963), with *Music and Phonorecords* as volumes 51-52
of the set (of which the latter volume is the subject index) and *1963-1967*
(67 vols., with *Music and Phonorecords* forming a three-volume set, of which
volume 3 is a subject index; Ann Arbor: Edwards, 1969). It should be
emphasized that the *Music and Phonorecords* volumes include not only these
categories of publications, but also libretti and books about music and musicians.
The *National Union Catalog, 1956 through 1967* (Totowa, N.J.: Rowman and
Littlefield, [1970-]) forms a cumulation of the 1958-62 and 1963-67
quinquennial supplements. Library location of titles is further aided by the
*National Union Catalog . . . Register of Additional Locations* (Washington:
Library of Congress, 1965-). National coverage has been extended into the
past by the publication of *The National Union Catalog, 1952-1955 Imprints*
(30 vols.; Ann Arbor: Edwards, 1961). The Library of Congress catalogues and
the *National Union Catalog* through the 1953-57 cumulation will eventually be
superseded by *The National Union Catalog, Pre-1956 Imprints; A Cumulative
Author List Representing Library of Congress Printed Cards and Titles Reported
by Other American Libraries* ([Chicago]: Mansell, 1968-), but without the
inclusion of phonorecords. In 1973 the title of *Music and Phonorecords* was
changed to *Music, Books on Music, and Sound Recordings.*

There are also subject catalogues to the Library of Congress collections. These are represented by the cumulation volumes *Library of Congress Catalog . . . Books: Subjects, 1950-1954* (20 vols.; Ann Arbor: Edwards, 1955), *1955-1959* (22 vols.; Paterson, N.J.: Pageant, 1960), *1960-1964* (25 vols.; Ann Arbor: Edwards, 1965), *1965-1969* (42 vols.; Ann Arbor: Edwards, 1970), as well as by quarterly and annual supplements. Certain of these publications reflect extended sections on music, with appropriate subheadings.

The Center for Research Libraries in Chicago (formerly the Midwest Inter-Library Center) is maintained for the purpose of increasing library materials available to its member (mostly universities in the United States and Canada). Its loose-leaf *Handbook* [Chicago: Center for Research Libraries, 1969] is on deposit in member libraries. Areas of concentration of interest to the music historian are archives, black studies, dissertations, literature and culture, newspapers, and religion. Published catalogues include *Catalogue: Monographs* (5 vols.; Chicago: Center for Research Libraries, 1969-70), *Catalogue: Newspapers* (1969), and *Catalogue: Serials* (2 vols.; 1972).

The Department of Printed Books of the British Museum in London has published very comprehensive catalogues of its collections. Earlier publications are generally superseded by the *General Catalogue of Printed Books* (263 vols.; London: Trustees, 1959-65). Contrary to the Library of Congress format, subject entries are incorporated here, at least to a limited extent, enhancing the bibliographical value of the set. Further attributes of this catalogue are the analyses of series and a large number of cross references, although imprint information is generally not as full as in the Library of Congress catalogues. The first decennial supplement issued by the Department is the *General Catalogue of Printed Books; Ten-Year Supplement, 1956-1965* (50 vols.; London: Trustees, 1968), which cumulates the annual volumes of additions. Subject control of the Museum's book collections is provided through the *Subject Index of the Modern Works Added to the Library, 1881-1900* (3 vols.; London: British Museum, 1902-3), edited by G. K. Fortescue. Supplements are available to this set, which itself continues the Peddie *Subject Index* (cf. Chapter VII).

The Bibliothèque Nationale in Paris has issued a *Catalogue général des livres imprimés, Auteurs* (Paris: Imprimerie Nationale, 1897-) and a *Catalogue général des livres imprimés: Auteurs—collectivité-auteurs—anonymes, 1960-1964* (Paris: Bibliothèque Nationale, 1965-). The later volumes of the former set include the note "Ouvrages publiés avant 1960." The latter set lists post-1959 imprints as well as some pre-1960 titles.

For Germany the chief catalogue is the *Deutscher Gesamtkatalog,* published by the Preussische Staatsbibliothek (14 vols., A-Beethordnung only; Berlin: Preussische Druckerei- u. Verlags-Aktiongesellschaft, 1931-39). This may be supplemented by the *Deutscher Gesamtkatalog, Neue Titel* (Berlin: Staatsbibliothek, 1893). The national union catalogue for Italy is the *Primo catalogo collettivo delle biblioteche italiane* (Roma: Centro Nazionale per il Catalogo Unico delle Biblioteche Italiane e per le Informazioni Bibliografiche, 1962-).

## Library Manuscript Catalogues

An invaluable universal guide to manuscript collections and their catalogues is Paul O. Kristeller's *Latin Manuscript Books Before 1600; A List of the Printed Catalogues and Unpublished Inventories of Extant Collections* (3rd ed.; New York: Fordham University Press, [1965]). Since in this section space can be given to only a few of the most outstanding catalogues for national collections and libraries, the work by Kristeller, which is not nearly as restrictive as the title implies, should be kept in mind as a further resource for this type of material, particularly for the indication of libraries containing unpublished inventories.

Reference may also be made to the earlier and less comprehensive *Unpublished Bibliographical Tools in Certain Archives and Libraries of Europe; A Partial List* (Washington: U.S. Library of Congress, 1952), compiled by Lester K. Born, which covers Austria, Belgium, England, France, Germany, the Netherlands, Scotland, and Switzerland. Certain volumes of the *Union World Catalogue of Manuscript Books* (New York: Wilson, 1933-) yield information on manuscript collections of the world, particularly volumes 1 (*The World's Collections of Manuscript Books; A Preliminary Survey*), 2 (*The Manuscript Book Collections of Spain and Portugal,* with a supplement in volume 5), and 3 (*A List of Printed Catalogs of Manuscript Books*).

A universal catalogue of manuscripts which is now quite old and in large part superseded by other material is Louis de Mas-Latrie's *Dictionnaire des manuscrits, ou recueil de catalogues de manuscrits* (2 vols.; Paris: Migne, 1853). This work, which concentrates largely on ecclesiastical and historical material, is organized by country, with the entire of volume 1 devoted to France. Finally, the periodical *Scriptorium* [1946/47-] provides a wealth of information on manuscripts. The journal's index is very detailed, indicating among other things the name of the holding library and the presence of music in the manuscript.

European national libraries not brought out in the following pages either are not represented by manuscript catalogues or contain collections so fragmented that the detailing of their catalogues would demand an inordinate amount of space.

Seymour de Ricci and W. J. Wilson, *Census of Medieval and Renaissance Manuscripts in the United States and Canada* (3 vols.; New York: [various publishers], 1935-62) remains the standard work for these countries. Collections in the United States are recorded in Philip M. Hamer's *A Guide to Archives and Manuscripts in the United States* (New Haven: Yale University Press, 1961) and in the *National Union Catalog of Manuscript Collections* [1959/61-] ([place varies: various publishers], 1962-). The 1968 volume of the latter title contains "Repositories Represented in the National Union Catalog of Manuscript Collections, 1959-1968." Musical interests are delineated by index references such as "Musicians" or "Musical Societies." Guides to the Library of Congress Manuscript Division include, among others, the *Handbook of Manuscripts in the Library of Congress* (Washington: Government Printing Office, 1918). Bibliographical control of manuscripts in Canada is afforded through the *Union List of Manuscripts in Canadian Repositories / Catalogue collectif des manuscrits des archives canadiennes* (Ottawa: Public Archives of Canada, 1968). Although this has a detailed index, the latter is directed to persons, rather than subjects.

Manuscripts in British libraries are detailed in several works.[3] In chronological order these are Edward Bernard, *Catalogi librorum manuscriptorum Angliae et Hiberniae* (2 vols.; Oxford: E Teatro Sheldoniano, 1697), Beriah Botfield, *Notes on the Cathedral Libraries of England* (London: [Pickering], 1849), and Neil R. Ker, *Medieval Manuscripts in British Libraries* (Oxford: Clarendon Press, 1969-). Despite the age of the first-named work, it is still invaluable for holdings of cathedral libraries, which in Great Britain are important repositories of music.

The British Museum has issued a large number of catalogues of its manuscript collections, to which T. C. Skeat, *The Catalogues of the Manuscript Collections* (rev. ed.; London: British Museum, 1962) is the guide. Music is covered *passim* in this fascinating volume. The following selection represents those catalogues of most interest to the music scholar.[4] Catalogues are S. Ayscough, *A Catalogue of the Manuscripts . . . Hitherto Undescribed* (2 vols.; London: Rivington, 1782), *Index to the Additional Manuscripts, with Those of the Egerton Collection . . . Acquired in the Years 1783-1835* (1849), *List of Additions to the Manuscripts in the British Museum* [1836-40] (1843), *Catalogue of Additions to the Manuscripts in the British Museum* [1841-53] (3 vols., includes Additional and Egerton manuscripts; 1850-68), *Catalogue of Manuscripts in the British Museum, New Series* (3 parts, listing Arundel and Burney manuscripts; 1834-41), *Catalogue of Western Manuscripts in the Old Royal and King's Collections* (4 vols.; 1921), *A Catalogue of the Manuscripts in the Cottonian Library* (1802), *Catalogue of the Stowe Manuscripts* (2 vols.; 1895-96), *Catalogue of the Harleian Manuscripts in the British Museum* (4 vols.; 1808-12), and *A Catalogue of the Lansdowne Manuscripts* (1819).

---

[3] Lester K. Born's *British Manuscripts Project; A Checklist of the Microfilms Prepared in England and Wales for the American Council of Learned Societies, 1941-1945* (Washington: Library of Congress, 1955) lists films of manuscripts and early prints available at the Library of Congress.

[4] Where no place and publisher are given for titles in the following selection, it may be assumed that they are London and British Museum.

Two series of catalogues disclose the holdings of the National Library of Wales. These are the *Catalogue of Manuscripts* (Aberystwyth: National Library, 1921-) and the *Handlist of Manuscripts in the National Library of Wales* ([Aberystwyth: National Library of Wales, 1940-]). The National Library of Scotland, which owes its origin to the Advocates' Library, is represented by the *Catalogue of Manuscripts Acquired Since 1925* (Edinburgh: National Library of Scotland, 1938-) and *Scottish Manuscripts* (Edinburgh: National Library of Scotland, 1967), although the most valuable catalogues are in the library itself in manuscript form.

France is well represented by the two series *Catalogue général des manuscrits des Bibliothèques Publiques des Départements* (7 vols., Quarto series; Paris: Imprimerie Nationale, 1849-85) and *Catalogue général des manuscrits des Bibliothèques Publiques de France, Départements* (Octavo Series; Paris: Plon-Nourrit et Cie, 1886-). A guide to the catalogues of the Bibliotheque Nationale is *Les Catalogues imprimés de la Bibliothèque Nationale* (Paris: Bibliothèque Nationale, 1953), in which music is strongly represented. The general manuscript catalogues of this library are for the most part organized according to the language of the manuscript groups. French manuscripts of the Bibliothèque Nationale may be found listed in the *Catalogue général des manuscrits français* (18 vols.; Paris: [various publishers], 1868-1918), which has the following subseries:

| Series | | Volume | Number |
|---|---|---|---|
| I | Ancien fonds français | 1-5 | 1-6170 |
| II | Ancien supplément français | 1-3 | 6171-15369 |
| III | Ancien Saint-German français | 1-3 | 15370-20064 |
| IV | Ancien petits fonds français | 1-3 | 20065-33264 |
| V | Nouv. acquis. françaises | 1-4 | 1-11353; 20001-22811 |

A *Table générale alphabétique* for subseries I-IV and V in part was published 1931-48 in six volumes. The Latin manuscripts are recorded, with indexes, in the *Catalogue général des manuscrits latins* (Paris: Bibliothèque Nationale, 1939-), while the English-language manuscripts are described in the *Catalogue du manuscrits anglais de la Bibliothèque nationale* (Paris: Champion, 1884), by Gaston Raynaud. Space does not permit the naming of the many other catalogues for manuscripts in the for manuscripts in the Bibliothèque Nationale, but the reader is referred to the above-named *Catalogues imprimés de la Bibliothèque Nationale* for details.

The manuscripts of the Bibliothèque Nationale of the Grand Duchy of Luxembourg are registered in the *Catalogue des livres et des manuscrits de la Bibliothèque de Luxembourg* (Luxembourg: Lamort, 1846) or in N. van Werveke, *Catalogue descriptif des manuscrits de la Bibliothèque de Luxembourg* (Luxembourg: Bourg-Bourger, 1894). A bibliographical aid to Belgian manuscript is Paul Faider, *Bibliographie des catalogues des manuscrits des Bibliothèques de Belgique* (Bruges: Imprimerie Sainte-Catharine, 1933). Manuscripts throughout Belgium are recorded in the *Catalogue général des manuscrits des bibliothèques de Belgique* (6 vols.; Gembloux: Duculot, 1934-50), while those in the Royal Library are listed in the *Catalogue des manuscrits de la Bibliothèque Royale de Belgique* (13 vols.; Bruxelles: Lamertin, 1901-48).

Two important collections of manuscripts in the Biblioteca nacional in Lisbon are represented by the catalogues *Os codices alcobacenses da Biblioteca nacional* (Lisboa: Biblioteca nacional, 1926-) and *Inventario, seccão XIII-manuscriptos; Collecção Pombalina* (Lisboa: [Biblioteca Nacional], 1889). Spanish manuscripts are described in José María de Eguren, *Memoria descriptiva de los códices notables conservados en los Archivos Eclesiásticos de Espanã* (Madrid: Rivadeneyra, 1859). The National Library manuscripts are recorded in the *Inventario general de manuscritos de la Biblioteca Nacional* (Madrid: Ministerio de Educacion Nacional, 1953-).

Italy is covered in the monumental series by Giuseppe Mazzatinti and A. Sorbelli, *Inventari dei manoscritti delle bibliotheche d'Italia* ([place varies: various publishers, 1890-]). In volume 21 an index to the preceding volumes may be found, but Kristeller gives a more complete listing of the contents. One should also see the latter's *Iter Italicum* (2 vols.; London/Leiden: Warburg Institute, 1963-67), which is a finding list of uncatalogued or incompletely catalogued humanistic manuscripts of the Renaissance in Italian and other libraries. Several large cities in Italy possess their own "national" library. For the Biblioteca Nazionale Centrale Vittorio Emanuele II in Rome we have *I manoscritti Capilupiani della Biblioteca Nazionale Centrale di Roma* (Roma: La Libreria dello Stato, 1939), by Tullia Gasparrini Leporace, as well as an important unpublished inventory.[5] Manuscripts in the Biblioteca Nazionale Centrale in Florence are recorded in two catalogues by Adolfo Bartoli. The first of these is *I manoscritti italiani della Biblioteca Nazionale di Firenze* (4 vols.; Firenze: [privately printed], 1879-85), and the second is *Cataloghi dei manoscritti della R. Biblioteca Nazionale Centrale di Firenze* (Roma: Ministerio della Pubblica Istruzione, 1889-). Beyond these, "Fondi" such as the Palatini, the Panciatichiani, and the Foscoliani are accorded their own catalogues. The general manuscripts of the Biblioteca Nazionale Universitaria in Turin are registered in *Codices manuscripti Bibliothecae regii taurinensis athenaei* (2 vols.; Taurini: Ex Typographia Regia, 1794), while the important Fondo Bobbio manuscripts are listed in *Codici bobbiesi nella Biblioteca nazionale di Torino* (Torino-Palermo: Clausen, 1890), by Giuseppe Ottino, and *Codici bobbiesi della Biblioteca nazionale universitaria di Torino* (2 vols.; Milano: Hoepli, 1907), by Carlo Cipolla. Inventories for the Biblioteca Nazionale Marciana in Venice are

---

5 Cf. Kristeller, *Latin Manuscript Books Before 1600*, p. 188.

J. Valentinelli's *Bibliotheca Manuscripta ad S. Marci Venetiarum* (6 vols.;
Venezia: [privately printed], 1868-73) and *Catalogo dei codici Marciani
Italiani* (2 vols.; Modena: Ferraguti, 1909-11), by Carlo Frati and Arnaldo
Segarizzi. Catalogues for the manuscripts in the Biblioteca Nazionale Braidense
in Milan, the Biblioteca Nazionale Vittorio Emanuele III in Naples, and the
Biblioteca Nazionale in Palermo are largely unpublished.

The older catalogue of the manuscripts at the Vatican library, *Bibliothecae
apostolicae vaticanae codicum manuscriptorum catalogus* (3 vols.; Romae:
Ex Typographia Linguarum Orientalium Angeli Rotilii in Aedibus Maximorum,
1756-59) has been for the most part superseded by specialized catalogues.[6]
Important catalogues are *Codices Vaticani Graeci* (4 vols.; 1923-50), *Codices
Graeci Chisiani et Borgiani* (1927), *Codices manuscripti Palatini Graeci* (1885),
*I codici Capponiani* (1897), *Codices Ferrajoli* (3 vols.; 1939-60), *Codices
Reginensis Latini* (2 vols.; 1937-45), *Codices Vrbinates Latini* (3 vols.; 1902-21),
*Codices Vaticani Latini* (1902-), and *Codices Palatini Latini* (volume 1 only,
to number 921; 1886). Kristeller, in his *Latin Manuscript Books Before 1600,*
lists general guides to the Vatican manuscript collections and gives bibliographical
references to the Knights of Columbus Vatican Film Library at Saint Louis
University, the latter being of special interest to the American scholar.

The Schweizerische Landesbibliothek / Bibliothèque nationale suisse /
Biblioteca nazionale svizzera in Berne posseses a relatively small manuscript
collection. The more comprehensive collections in Switzerland are found in
the cities of Basle, Geneva, and Zurich.

Manuscripts in various parts of Austria are recorded in the *Handschriftenver-
zeichnisse österreichischer Bibliotheken* ([place varies: various publishers], 1927-)
To date this series covers Kärnten and Steiermark. The Österreichische National-
bibliothek in Vienna has issued a splendid catalogue entitled *Tabvlae codicvm
manv scriptorvm . . . in Bibliotheca Palatina Vindobonensi asservatorvm* (11 vols.;
Vindobonae: venvm dat C. Geroldi filivs, 1864-1912). Volumes 9 and 10
contain the music manuscripts. Further, one should consult Otto Mazal and
Franz Unterkircher, *Katalog der abendländischen Handschriften der
Österreichischen Nationalbibliothek, "Series Nova" (Neuerwerbungen)*
(Vienna: Prachner, 1963-).

Germany is represented by two incomplete manuscript catalogue series. The
first of these is the *Verzeichniss der Handschriften im Preussischen Staate*
(3 vols.; Berlin: Bath, 1893-94), which lists holdings of the Göttingen
Universitäts-Bibliothek only. This series was followed by the *Verzeichnis der
Handschriften im Deutschen Reich* (3 vols.; Leipzig: Harrassowitz, 1938-44),
which lists manuscripts at Breslau, Graz, and in a special collection (the Jaina
Handschriften) at the former Preussische Staatsbibliothek, now the Deutsche

---

[6] Place and publisher in the following selection are The Vatican.

Staatsbibliothek. To some extent this series overlaps with the *Handschriften-verzeichnisse österreichischer Bibliotheken,* mentioned above. A rather unique inventory has been published which records manuscript collections of individual scholars and others in the Federal Republic and indicates where these are preserved. This is Ludwig Denecke's *Die Nachlässe in den Bibliotheken der Bundesrepublik Deutschland* (Boppard am Rhein: Boldt, [c1969]), whose index reflects a large number of musicians. The monumental catalogue for the manuscripts at the Deutsche Staatsbibliothek is *Handschriften-Verzeichnisse der Königlichen Bibliothek zu Berlin* (Berlin: [various publishers], 1853-). The manuscripts in this catalogue are arranged largely by language groups.

The manuscripts of the Dutch Koninklijke Bibliotheek in The Hague are recorded in the *Catalogus codicum manuscriptorum Bibliothecae Regiae* (Hagae Comitum: [Koninklijke Bibliotheek], 1922-). The *Catalogus codicum latinorum medii aevi Bibliothecae Regiae Hafniensis* (Hafniae: In Aedibus Gyldendalianis, 1926) lists Latin manuscripts in the Danish Royal Library, while French medieval manuscripts are found in *Description des manuscrits français du moyen âge de la Bibliothèque royale de Copenhague* (Copenhague: Thiele, 1844), by N. C. L. Abrahams, and the Scandinavian manuscripts may be located through the *Katalog over danske og norske digteres originalmanuskripter i det Kongelige Bibliotek* (Kϕbenhavn: Munksgaard, 1943), by Lauritz Nielsen. For Norway one is directed to the Universitets biblioteket in Oslo, which serves as a national depository. The Kungliga biblioteket in Stockholm is represented by an unfortunately incomplete *Kataloger över Kungl. bibliotekets i Stockholm handskrifter* (Stockholm: [Kungliga Biblioteket], 1923-), but there exists in the Library itself an inventory for medieval Swedish manuscripts by Gunnar Olof Hyltén-Cavallius. In Helsinki the Yliopiston kirjasto, or University Library, functions as a national library. Certain medieval manuscripts are covered by Toivo Haapanen's *Verzeichnis der mittelalterlichen Handschriftenfragmente in der Universitätsbibliothek zu Helsingfors* (3 vols.; Helsingfors: [Yliopiston Kirjasto], 1922-32), which concentrates on liturgical works.

For the Soviet Union two valuable library guides are Paul L. Horecky, *Libraries and Bibliographic Centers in the Soviet Union* (vol. 16, Indiana University Publications, Slavic and East European Series; Washington: Council on Library Resources, c1959) and Patricia K. Grimsted, *Archives and Manuscript Repositories in the USSR* (Princeton: Princeton University Press, c1972). The latter concentrates on Moscow and Leningrad, and the index contains references to "music libraries" and "materials relating to music." For the Otdel rukopiseĭ [manuscript division] of the Gosudarstvennaia ordena Lenina biblioteka SSSR imeni V. I. Lenina in Moscow there are internal handwritten inventories. Beyond this use may be made of the division's *Zapiski* [reports] (Moskva: Publichnaia Biblioteka, 1938-), the *Muzeĭnoe sobranie rukopiseĭ, Opisanie* (Moskva: Ministerstvo Kul'tur'i, 1961-), or the *Kratkiĭ ukazatel' arkhivnykh fondov otdela rukopiseĭ* (Moskva: Gosudarstvennaia Ordena Lenina Biblioteka SSSR, 1948). The old Imperial Public Library in Leningrad is now called the Gosudarstvennaia ordena Trudovogo Krasnogo Znameni publichnaia biblioteka imeni M. E. Saltykova-Shchedrina. Coverage for the nineteenth century is afforded in the *Istoria Gosudarstvennoi ordena Trudovogo Krasnogo Znameni publichnoi biblioteki imeni M. E. Saltykova-Shchedrina* (Leningrad: Lenizdat, 1963), while the four volumes of the *Kratkiĭ otchet* (Leningrad: Gosudarstvennaia Ordena Trudovogo Krasnogo Znameni Publichnaia Biblioteka, 1940-53) cover the period 1914 to 1951, superseded by *Novye postupleniia v otdele rukopiseĭ (1952-1966); Kratkiĭ otchet* (Moskva: Izd-vo "Kniga," 1968).[7] The excellent volume by Grimsted provides further details, particularly on individual manuscript groups.

Catalogues of various manuscript collections in Poland are given in K. Aland's *Die Handschriftenbestände der Polnischen Bibliotheken insbesondere an griechischen und lateinischen Handschriften* (Berlin: Akademie-Verlag, 1956). The National Library in Warsaw, which suffered great losses in World War II, is represented by the *Katalog rękopisów Bibljoteki Narodewej* (Warszawa: Bibjoteka Narodowa, 1929- ). Manuscript research in Czechoslovakia may be furthered through use of the *Soupis Rukopisů Knihoven a Archivů Zemí Českých, Jakož i Rukopisných Bohemik Mimočeských* (4 vols.; Prague: [privately printed], 1910-22). Two fine manuscript collections have been joined in the Státni knihovna ČSSR–Universitní knihovna in Prague. For the latter collection there exist two catalogues by J. Truhlář. *Catalogus codicum manuscriptorum latinorum qui in C. R. Bibliotheca Publica atque Universitatis Pragensis asservantur* (2 vols.; Praha: [privately printed], 1905-6) and *Katalog Českých Rukopisů c. k. Veřejné a Universitní Knihovny Pražské* (Praha: [privately printed], 1906), as well as a catalogue by Emma Urbánsková, *Rukopisy a Vzácné Tisky Pražské Universitní Knihovny* ([Praha]: Státni Pedagogicke Nakl., 1957). The national collection found in the Národní muzeum–Historické muzeum now includes important units which were once private or monastic.

Volume 12 of the *Catalogus Bibliothecae Musei Nationalis Hungarici* is *Codices latini medii aevi* (Budapestini: Sumptibus Musei Nationalis Hungarici, 1940), describing manuscripts in the Magyar Nemzeti Múzeum in Budapest. Manuscripts in the Országos Széchényi Könyvtár are represented in the older *Catalogus manuscriptorum Bibliothecae nationalis hungaricae Széchényiano-regnicolaris* (3 vols.; Sopronii: Typis Haeredom Siessianorum, 1814-15). Libraries in Bucharest, such as the Biblioteca Centrală de Stat and the Biblioteca Academiei, contain their own internal inventories.

---

[7] The English language reader is referred to Olga Golubeva, "The Saltykov-Shchedrin Library, Leningrad," *The Book Collector* IV (1955), 99-109.

The situation in Yugoslavia somewhat parallels that in Italy, but on a more limited scale. In the former country there are at least three "national" libraries, the Narodna Biblioteka in Belgrade, the Narodna in univerzitetna knijižnica in Ljubljana, and the Nacionalna i sveučilišna in Zagreb. For all three there are internal inventories, but in the case of the Zagreb library there is also an exhibit catalogue entitled *Izložba jugoslovenskih rukopisa i knjiga od XI.-XVIII. stoljeća, rujan 1954; Katalog* (Zagreb: Savez društava Bibliothekara Federativne Narodne Republike Jugoslavije, 1954). The Darzavna Biblioteka "Vassil Kolarov" in Sofia earlier went under the name Narodna biblioteka. Besides the catalogue for Slavic manuscripts by Ben'o Tsonev, *Opis na rŭkopisitie i staropechatnitie knigi* (Sofia: [Narodna Biblioteka], 1910), there are inventories within the library for other types of manuscripts. The manuscripts of the Ethnikē bibliothēkē in Athens are recorded in the *Katalogos* (Athenai: [Ethnikē Bibliothēkē], 1892), by I. and A. Sakkelion.

# CHAPTER X / Indexes and Editions of Vocal Texts

ONE OF THE MOST difficult tasks facing the editor of vocal works of the medieval and Renaissance periods is the editing of the verbal texts for that music. Although for the final editing the scholar may wish to draw on the expertise of the specialist in the language in question, this step may be prepared (or perhaps avoided entirely) if the editor is aware of the numerous sources which may contain an edited version of the text.

In the past, this information has largely been handed down in seminars or in communications between teacher and student. At this point it seems useful to list and comment on at least the major sources for the basic languages and literatures with which the musicologist has to deal. Through the use of the following references, other, perhaps older, sources may be brought to the reader's attention. There is certainly no claim to completeness here.

In the ensuing discussion bibliographies or indexes will be treated first, followed by editions of the texts. Collections entirely by one author or from one manuscript are omitted, since these are more approachable through conventional bibliographies. Collections of texts with music are also excluded as far as practicable, for the editor will be, for the most part, aware of these. One-volume anthologies without particular subject or chronological orientation are largely ignored, for they seldom reflect the necessary specialization.

Frequent reference is made in the following pages to large sets or series of literary importance but no attempt is made to analyze these beyond the citation of one or two titles to exemplify contents.[1] Additional bibliographical aid, particularly in the matter of texts by one author, may be obtained through recourse to appropriate titles brought out in Chapter VII of the present work.

## Latin Texts

In addition to those bibliographies cited in Chapter VII which direct themselves to medieval studies and to literature separately, there are certain literary studies

---

[1] Volume analytics to large series can be found in the work by Eleanora A. Baer referred to in Chapter VII.

which may be of aid to the area now in question. Those with particularly fine bibliographies are Ernst Robert Curtius, *European Literature and the Latin Middle Ages,* translated by Willard R. Trask ( [New York] : Pantheon Books [1953] ); Martin R. P. McGuire, *Introduction to Mediaeval Latin Studies* (Washington, D.C.: Catholic University of America Press, 1964); Karl Strecker, *Introduction to Medieval Latin,* translated by Robert B. Palmer (4. Auflage; Dublin: Weidmann, 1967); and the older *Geschichte der lateinischen Literatur des Mittelalters* (3 vols.; München: Beck, 1911-31), by Max Manitius.

Two publications by Hanns Bohatta catalogue printed breviaries and missals, respectively. These are *Bibliographie der Breviere, 1501-1850* (Leipzig: Hiersemann, 1937) and *Catalogus missalium ritus latini ab anno M.CCCC.LXXIV impressorum* (London: Quaritch, 1928), the latter co-authored by William H. J. Weale.

An index of liturgical texts drawn from the Scriptures is Carl Marbach's *Carmina Scripturarum, scilicet antiphonas et responsoria ex Sacro Scripturae fonte in libros liturgicos Sanctae Ecclesiae Romanae derivata* (Strassburg: Le Roux, 1907). The immediate Scriptural source is indicated, and some immediate post-Biblical material is appended. Generally non-Scriptural material, with references to editions, is indexed in Cyr Ulysse Joseph Chevalier, *Repertorium hymnologicum; Catalogue des chants, hymnes, proses, séquences, tropes en usage dans l'église latine depuis les origines jusqu'à nos jours* (6 vols.; Louvain et Bruxelles: Soc. des Bollandistes, 1892-1920). Occasionally concordances may be of aid in Scriptural references; such a one for the Latin Bible is *Concordantiarum universae Scripturae Sacrae thesaurus ea methodo qua P. de Raze disposuit suum Concordantiarum SS. Scripturae manuale* (Paris: Lethielleux, 1939). Older hymn material is listed in James Mearns's *Early Latin Hymns; An Index of Hymns in Hymnaries Before 1100, with an Appendix from Later Sources* (Cambridge: University Press, 1913).

Dom René-Jean Hesbert has provided texts of six older Graduals and Antiphonals, respectively, in his *Antiphonale Missarum sextuplex* (Bruxelles: Vromant, 1935) and in his *Corpus antiphonalium officii* (3 vols.; Roma: Herder, 1963-68). The texts are arranged in parallel columns. Dom Prosper Guéranger's *The Liturgical Year,* translated by Dom Laurence Shepherd (15 vols.; Westminster, Md.: Newman Press, 1948-50) is a valuable repository of propers, prayers, antiphons, hymns, tropes, and other similar textual material in Latin, with English translation, not only from the Roman rite, but also from Byzantine, Ambrosian, Gallican, and Mozarabic sources. Within the particular season the approach is by the Proper of the Time, followed by the Proper of the Saints. The series is replete with explanatory discussion, but unfortunately there is no index.

A major collection of medieval ecclesiastical texts is the *Analecta hymnica medii aevi* (55 vols.; Leipzig: Reisland, 1886-1922), compiled by Guido Maria

Dreves, Clemens Blume, and others.[2] Besides newer compilations, older editions
are revised in this magnificent series. A selection of texts from the publication
is presented in G. M. Dreves and Clemens Blume, *Ein Jahrtausend lateinischer
Hymnendichtung* (2 vols.; Leipzig: Reisland, 1909). Henry Adalbert Daniel's
*Thesaurus hymnologicus; Sive hymnorum, canticorum, sequentiarum circa
annum MD usitarum collectio amplissima* (5 vols.; Leipzig: Loeschke, 1855-62)
is perhaps the largest of the collections revised in the *Analecta hymnica medii
aevi.* The *Texte und Untersuchungen zur Geschichte der altchristlichen
Literatur* (in four series; Leipzig: Hinrichs, 1882-) contains, among other things,
the *Passio S. Theclae Virginis.*

Smaller collections are Franz Joseph Mone, *Lateinische Hymnen des Mittelalters* (3 vols.; Freiburg im Breisgau: Herder, 1853-55) and Gall Morel,
*Lateinische Hymnen des Mittelalters* (2 vols.; Einsiedeln: Benziger, 1866-68),
the latter containing Swiss texts. Gustav Milchsack's *Hymni et sequentiae cum
aliis et Latinis et Gallicis necnon Theotiscis carminibus medio aevo compositis*
(Halle: [privately printed], 1886) presents the medieval collection of the
sixteenth-century compiler Matthias Flacius Illyricus called "Carmina vetusta
ante 300 annos scripta." Following on this are F. Wilhelm Emil Roth's
*Lateinische Hymnen des Mittelalters* (Augsburg: Schmid, 1888) and E. Misset
and W. H. J. Weale's *Analecta liturgica* (2 vols.; Insulis et Brugis: Typis Societatis
S. Augustini, 1888-92), the second part of which is entitled *Thesaurus
hymnologicus.* Further titles are Ad. Schulte, *Die Hymnen des Breviers nebst
den Sequenzen des Missale* (Paderborn: Schöningh, 1898); A. S. Walpole,
*Early Latin Hymns* (Cambridge: The University Press, 1922); Dom Matthew
Britt, *The Hymns of the Breviary and Missal* (New York: Benziger, 1948);
Gottfried Schille, *Frühchristliche Hymnen* (Berlin: Evangelische Verlagsanstalt,
1962); and Josef Szövérffy, *Die Annalen der lateinischen Hymnendichtung;
Ein Handbuch* (2 vols.; Berlin: Schmidt, [1964-65]). The Walpole volume
contains an index of first lines and an "index of words."

Sequences, tropes, proses, and allied material are covered in Ferdinand J.
Wolf, *Ueber die Lais, Sequenzen und Leiche* (Heidelberg: Winter, 1841), John
M. Neale, *Sequentiae ex missalibus Germanicis, Anglicis, Gallicis aliisque medii
aevi collectae* (London: Parker, 1852), and Karl Bartsch, *Die lateinischen
Sequenzen des Mittelalters in musikalischer und rhythmischer Beziehung*
(Rostock: Stiller'sche Hofbuchhandlung, 1868). Joseph Kehrein's *Lateinische
Sequenzen des Mittelalters, aus Handschriften und Drucke* (Mainz: Kupferberg,
1873) provides an index of first lines. Further resources are Adam Reiners,
*Die Tropen-, Prosen- und Präfations-Gesänge des feierlichen Hochamtes im
Mittelalter* (Luxemburg: Hary, 1884), Gustaf Edward Klemming, *Hymni,*

---

2 Contents by volume are listed in Bruno Stäblein, "Analecta hymnica medii aevi,"
*Die Musik in Geschichte und Gegenwart,* ed. by Friedrich Blume (Kassel: Bärenreiter,
1949-), I, 446-49.

*Sequentiae et piae cantiones in Regno Sueciae olim usitate* (Stockholm:
Norstedt, 1885), Léon Gautier, *Histoire de la poésie liturgique au moyen age
[sic]; Les tropes* (Paris: Palmé, 1886), and Nikolaus Gihr, *Die Sequenzen des
römischen Messbuches* (Freiburg i. Br.: Heder'sche Verlagshandlung, 1887).
The Gautier volume lists tropes for the Kyrie, Gloria, and Regnum, and gives
scattered bibliography or editions of tropes.

Smaller collections, with subject or chronological orientation, include three
by Edeléstand P. du Méril, *Poésies populaires latines antérieures au douzième
siècle* (Paris: Brockhaus et Avenarius, 1843), *Poésies populaires latines du
moyen âge* (Paris: Didot, 1847), and *Poésies inédites du moyen âge* (Paris:
Franck, 1854). Further titles are Thomas Wright, *Anglo-Latin Satirical Poets
and Epigrammatists of the Twelfth Century* (London: Longman, 1872),
Edmond Faral, *Les arts poétiques du XII$^e$ et du XIII$^e$ siècles* (Paris: Champion,
1924), Robert Stroppel, *Liturgie und geistliche Dichtung zwischen 1050 und
1300* (Frankfurt a/M: Diesterweg, 1927), Dom André Wilmart, *Auteurs spirituels
et textes dévots du moyen âge latin* (Paris: Bloud et Gay, 1932), Helen Waddell,
*Medieval Latin Lyrics* (5th ed.; London: Constable, 1948), George F. Whicher,
*The Goliard Poets; Medieval Latin Songs and Satires* (New York: New Directions,
1965), and Edwin H. Zeydel, *Vagabond Verse; Secular Latin Poems of the Middle
Ages* (Detroit: Wayne State University Press, 1966). Some of these volumes
contain translations into the vernacular.

Two very comprehensive treatments of medieval drama are Edmund K.
Chambers, *The Medieval Stage* (2 vols.; Oxford: Clarendon Press, 1903) and
Karl Young, *The Drama of the Medieval Church* (2 vols.; Oxford: Clarendon
Press, 1933). These are also of bibliographical value. Volumes containing texts
are Achille Jubinal, *Mystères inédites du quinzième siècle* (Paris: Téchener,
1837), Thomas Wright, *Early Mysteries and Other Latin Poems of the Twelfth
and Thirteenth Centuries* (London: Nichols, 1838), Gustav Milchsack, *Die Oster-
und Passionsspiele* (Wolfenbüttel: Zwissler, 1879), Edeléstand P. du Méril, *Les
Origines latines du théatre modern* (Leipzig: Welter, 1897), and M. Sepet, *Les
Origines catholiques du théâtre modern* (Paris: Lethielleux, 1901).

Occasionally, sets which are not essentially literary may provide edited texts.
The Series Latina of Jacques Paul Migne's *Patrologia cursus completus, seu
bibliotheca universalis* (221 vols.; Paris: Garnier, 1844–1904) contains not only
lives, chronicles, and miracles, but also hymns and other poetic material. The
last four volumes of this monumental set form the index, but there is also
available an *Elucidatio in 235 tabulas* (Rotterdam: De Ford, 1952). The *Acta
Sanctorum, quotquot toto orbe coluntur* (cf. Chapter VI) contains legends
and biographies of the saints in chronological order by saints' days.
Volume 1 begins with January.[3] The *Corpus scriptorum ecclesiasticorum*

---

[3] For a description and the general contents of the original edition see August Potthast,
*Bibliotheca historica medii aevi* (2 vols., 2. Auflage; Berlin: Weber, 1896), I, xxxii–xxxiii.

*latinorum* ([place varies: various publishers], 1866-) is generally devoted to the writings of the Church Fathers, but volume 51 is *Aurelii Prudentii Clementis Carmina.* Two further ecclesiastical titles are the *Bibliotheca Patrum Latinorum Hispaniensis,* edited by Gustav Loewe and W. von Hartel (Wien: Tempsky, 1887), valuable for Spain, and the *Corpus Reformatorum* ([place varies: various publishers], 1834-), which has volumes devoted to the works of Melanchthon, Calvin, and Zwingli.

Two valuable historical series may be mentioned in this context. The *Rerum Britannicarum medii aevi scriptores; Or, Chronicles and Memorials of Great Britain and Ireland During the Middle Ages* (London: [various publishers], 1858-), known as the "Rolls Series," presents not only chronicles, histories, and memorials, but also poems, songs, and narratives.[4] There are many subseries to the *Monumenta Germaniae historica,* but perhaps that entitled *Poetarum Latinorum medii aevi* (Berlin: Weidmann, 1880-) would be most useful for our purposes. This subseries includes, for example, *Poetae latini aevi Carolini.* In addition, the *Henry Bradshaw Society Publications* ([London] : Harrison, 1890-) include British and other liturgical works such as the *Hereford Breviary.*

Latin texts with German language elements are the subject of three works edited by Karl Langosch: *Geistliche Spiele; Lateinische Dramen des Mittelalters mit deutschen Versen* (2. Auflage; Berlin: Rutten & Loening, [1957] ), *Hymnen und Vagantenlieder; Lateinische Lyrik des Mittelalters mit deutschen Versen* (Basel: Schwabe, [1954] ), and *Waltharius, Ruodlieb, Märchenepen; Lateinische Epik des Mittelalters mit deutschen Versen* (Basel: Schwabe, [1956] ). A volume with a similar approach is edited by Harry C. Schnur, *Lateinische Gedichte deutscher Humanisten; Lateinisch und Deutsch* (Stuttgart: Reclam, 1966).

## English Texts

In addition to those bibliographies of English literature brought out in Chapter VII, two should be mentioned here which are concerned exclusively with earlier periods of the literature. These are William Matthews, *Old and Middle English Literature* (New York: Appleton-Century-Crofts, 1968), designed for graduate and advanced undergraduate students, and Jonathan B. Severs, *A Manual of the Writings in Middle English, 1050-1500* (New Haven: Connecticut Academy of Arts and Sciences, 1967-). The latter is based on John E. Wells's *A Manual of the Writings in Middle English, 1050-1400* and presents a commentary and a bibliography for each piece of literature.

Two bibliographical titles which are of importance for the three strains of balladry are George M. Laws, *American Balladry from British Broadsides*

---

[4] An evaluation of the "Rolls Series" is provided in V. H. Galbraith, *An Introduction to the Use of the Public Records* (Oxford: Clarendon Press, 1934), pp. 71-72.

(Philadelphia: American Folklore Society, 1957) and Tristram P. Coffin, *The British Traditional Ballad in North America* (rev. ed.; Philadelphia: The American Folklore Society, 1963). The former lists the ballads by theme, with texts and editions, while the latter consists for the most part of a critical bibliographical study.

A valuable index of early English material is Carleton F. Brown and Rossell H. Robbins, *The Index of Middle English Verse* (New York: Index Society, 1943), which should be used with its supplement by Robbins and John L. Cutler (Lexington: University of Kentucky Press, 1965). Joseph Ritson's *Bibliographia poetica; A Catalog of English Poets of the Twelfth, Thirteenth, Fourteenth, Fifteenth, and Sixteenth Centurys* [sic] , *with a Short Account of Their Works* (London: Roworth, 1802) is organized by century and includes an appendix listing "Poets, Natives of Engleland [sic] , who wrote in Latin or French." Further indexes of poetry are Carleton F. Brown, *A Register of Middle English Religious and Didactic Verse* (2 vols.; Oxford: Bibliographical Society, 1916-20), whose second volume contains an index of first lines and an index of subjects and titles, and Margaret Crum, *First-Line Index of English Poetry, 1500-1800, in Manuscripts of the Bodleian Library, Oxford* (2 vols.; Oxford: Clarendon Press, 1969), a unique set with copious indexes. Folksongs and ballads, respectively, may be located in Margaret Dean-Smith's *A Guide to English Folk Song Collections, 1822-1952, with an Index to Their Contents, Historical Annotations, and an Introduction* (Liverpool: University Press, 1945), or in Hyder E. Rollins' *An Analytical Index to the Ballad Entries (1557-1709) in the Registers of the Company of Stationers of London* (Chapel Hill: University of North Carolina Press, 1924), the latter indexing by titles, first lines, and names and subjects.

For early plays one may wish to supplement the Gregor and Stratman titles given in Chapter VII with James O. Halliwell-Phillipps, *A Dictionary of Old English Plays, Existing Either in Print or in Manuscript, from the Earliest Times to the Close of the Seventeenth Century* (London: Smith, 1860). Edmund K. Chambers' *The Elizabethan Stage* (4 vols.; Oxford: Clarendon Press, 1923), although basically a critical work, does contain indexes of plays.

Two very large series which may be of considerable aid to the historian are the *Early English Text Society Publications,* which are divided into an "Original Series" (London: Early English Text Society, 1864-) and an "Extra Series" (126 nos.; London: Early English Text Society, 1867-1935), and the *Spenser Society Publications* (53 vols.; Manchester: Spenser Society, 1867-95). In the first-named one will find, for example, *The Salisbury Psalter,* while George Whither's *Hymns and Songs of the Church* forms a volume of the *Spenser Society Publications.*

Smaller but still rather general collections are Thomas Percy, *Reliques of Ancient English Poetry* (3 vols.; London: Dodsley, 1765); Joseph Ritson, *The*

*English Anthology* (3 vols.; London: Clarke, 1793-94); Sir Walter Scott's
*Minstrelsy of the Scottish Border,* edited by T. F. Henderson (4 vols.; Edinburgh:
Blackwood, 1902); and Edward Arber, *An English Garner,* edited by Thomas
Secombe (12 vols.; Westminster: Constable, 1903-4). Many of these contain
Middle English literature.

   Volumes falling into the period to about the year 1500 are Joseph Ritson,
*Ancient Engleish Metrical Romanceës* (3 vols.; London: Nicol, 1802), Ritson's
*Ancient Popular Poetry,* edited by Edmund Goldsmith (2 vols.; Edinburgh:
[privately printed], 1884), Edward Arber, *The Dunbar Anthology, 1401-1508
A.D.* (London: Frowde, 1901), Edmund K. Chambers and F. Sidgwick, *Early
English Lyrics, Amorous, Divine, Moral & Trivial* (London: Bullen, 1907),
Kenneth Sisam, *Fourteenth Century Verse and Prose* (London: Clarendon Press,
1921), Eleanor P. Hammond, *English Verse between Chaucer and Surrey*
(Durham, N.C.: Duke University Press, 1927), Carleton Brown, *English Lyrics
of the XIIIth Century* (Oxford: Clarendon Press, 1932), Brown's *Religious
Lyrics of the XVth Century* (Oxford: Clarendon Press, 1939), Bruce Dickens
and R. M. Wilson, *Early Middle English Texts* (New York: Norton, [1951]),
Carleton Brown, *Religious Lyrics of the XIVth Century* (2nd ed.; Oxford:
Clarendon Press, 1952), Rossell H. Robbins, *Secular Lyrics of the XIVth and
XVth Centuries* (Oxford: Clarendon Press, 1952), R. T. Davies, *Medieval
English Lyrics; A Critical Anthology* (London: Faber and Faber, [1963]),
J. A. W. Bennett and G. V. Smithers, *Early Middle English Verse and Prose*
(2nd ed.; Oxford: Clarendon Press, 1968), Ann S. Haskell, *A Middle English
Anthology* (Garden City, N.Y.: Anchor, 1969), and Celia Sisan, *Oxford Book
of Medieval English Verse* (London: Oxford University Press, 1970). Collections
devoted to historical or political verse are two by Thomas Wright, *Political
Poems and Songs Relating to English History, Composed During the Period
from the Accession of Edw. III to That of Ric. III* (2 vols.; London: Longman,
Green, Longman, and Roberts, 1859-61) and *The Political Songs of England
from the Reign of John to That of Edward II,* revised by Edmund Goldschmid
(4 vols.; Edinburgh: [privately printed], 1884) and Rossell H. Robbins'
*Historical Poems of the XIVth and XVth Centuries* (New York: Columbia
University Press, 1959).

   Collections extending from the late sixteenth to the early seventeenth century
are J. M. Berdan, *Early Tudor Poetry, 1485-1547* (New York: Macmillan, 1920),
Edmund K. Chambers, *The Oxford Book of Sixteenth Century Verse* (Oxford:
Clarendon Press, [1932]), Hyder E. Rollins, *Tottel's Miscellany (1557-1587)*
(2 vols., rev. ed.; Cambridge, Mass.: Harvard University Press, 1965), and Edmund
H. Fellowes, *English Madrigal Verse, 1588-1632* (3rd ed.; Oxford: Clarendon
Press, 1967). Volumes devoted to the Elizabethan period are four by Arthur
Henry Bullen, *More Lyrics from the Song-Books of the Elizabethan Age*
(London: Nimmo, 1888), *Poems, Chiefly Lyrical, from Romances and Prose*

*Tracts of the Elizabethan Age* (London: Nimmo, 1890), *Lyrics from the Song-Books of the Elizabethan Age* ([3rd ed.]; London: Lawrence and Bullen, 1893), and *Lyrics from the Dramatists of the Elizabethan Age* (London: Bullen, 1901), as well as Norman Ault's *Elizabethan Lyrics from the Original Texts* ([3rd ed.]; New York: Sloane, [1949]).

A major collection of seventeenth-century material is George Saintsbury's *Minor Poets of the Caroline Period* (3 vols.; Oxford: Clarendon Press, 1905-21). Further compilations are Arthur H. Bullen's *Musa proterva; Love Poems of the Restoration* (London: [Whittingham], 1889), Bullen's *Speculum amantis; Love Poems from Rare Song-Books and Miscellanies of the Seventeenth Century* ([London: Clay], 1902), H. J. C. Grierson, *The Oxford Book of Seventeenth Century Verse* (Oxford: Clarendon Press, 1934), and Norman Ault, *Seventeenth Century Lyrics* (2nd ed.; New York: Longmans, Green, [1950]).

Interest in the early English carol dates back to the nineteenth century, with primary attention being given to the Christmas carol. Some prominent collections of this genre are Thomas Wright, *Specimens of Old Christmas Carols, Selected from Manuscripts and Printed Books* (London: Richards, 1841), Arthur H. Bullen, *A Christmas Garland; Carols and Poems from the Fifteenth Century to the Present Time* (London: Nimmo, 1885), Edith Rickert, *Ancient English Christmas Carols, 1400-1700* (New York: Duffield, 1915), Richard L. Greene, *The Early English Carols* (Oxford: Clarendon Press, 1935), Rossell H. Robbins, *Early English Christmas Carols* (New York: Columbia University Press, 1961), and Richard L. Greene's *A Selection of English Carols* (Oxford: Clarendon Press, 1962).

The *Ballad Society Publications* (London: Taylor, 1868-) contain important collections of this species of literary endeavor, for example the *Roxburghe Ballads* in nine volumes. Some further groups are Thomas Percy, *The Percy Folio of Old English Ballads and Romances* (4 vols.; London: De La More, 1905-10), Andrew Clark, *The Shirburn Ballads, 1585-1616* (Oxford: Clarendon Press, 1907), and Hyder E. Rollins, *The Pepys Ballads* (8 vols.; Cambridge, Mass.: Harvard University Press, 1929-32). General collections of importance are Henry Huth, *Ancient Ballads and Broadsides Published in England in the Sixteenth Century* (London: Philobiblon Society, 1867); Joseph Ritson, *Ancient Songs and Ballads* (3rd ed.; London: Reeves and Turner, 1877); Francis James Child, *The English and Scottish Popular Ballads* (5 vols.; Boston and New York: Houghton, Mifflin, [1882-98]);[5] Hyder E. Rollins, *Old English Ballads, 1553-1625* (Cambridge: University Press, 1920), in which the ballads are arranged by subject, with an index of first lines, titles, and tunes; and Rollins' *Cavalier and Puritan; Ballads and Broadsides Illustrating the Period of the Great Rebellion, 1640-1660* (New York: New York University Press, 1923).

Since lyrical material is very often found within plays, some important collections of stage works may be brought out in concluding this section.

---

[5] The musician will want to consult Bertrand H. Bronson, *The Traditional Tunes of the Child Ballads* (Princeton: Princeton University Press, 1959-).

These are Joseph Q. Adams, *Chief Pre-Shakespearean Dramas* (London: Harrap, [no date]), a volume which presents a selection of plays from the origins of English drama to Shakespeare; Arthur H. Bullen, *A Collection of Old English Plays* (4 vols.; London: Wyman, 1882-85), of which also a "New Series" was brought out by the same publisher in the years 1887-90 in three volumes; John M. Manly, *Specimens of the Pre-Shakespearean Drama* (2 vols.; Boston: Ginn, 1897-98); Charles M. Gayley, *Representative English Comedies* (3 vols.; New York: Macmillan, 1903-14); and a large collection by Robert Dodsley entitled *A Select Collection of Old Plays* (15 vols.; London: Reeves and Turner, 1874-76).

## German Texts

As a supplement to the German bibliographies brought out in Chapter VII we might mention Johannes Hansel's *Bücherkunde für Germanisten* (5. Auflage; Berlin: Schmidt, 1968). This is a basic bibliography of indexes and criticism, with annotations.

The major listing of the literature itself is Karl Goedeke, *Grundriss zur Geschichte der deutschen Dichtung aus den Quellen* (2. Auflage, with supplements; Dresden: Ehlermann, 1884-). Goedeke's approach is from periods to categories (e.g., "Höfische Ritterdichtung") and then to individual figures or works. In addition to the Goedeke one may wish to consult Moriz Grolig, *Nicht bei Goedeke; Viertausend in Goedekes "Grundriss der deutschen Dichtung" fehlende Schriftsteller und Werke* (Wien: Krieg, [no date]). Wolfgang Stammler's *Die deutsche Literatur des Mittelalters; Verfasserlexikon* (5 vols.; Berlin: De Gruyter, 1933-55) embraces significant anonymous works and those in medieval Latin as well as the German literature. Occasionally line beginnings are provided. Herbert A. and Elisabeth Frenzel's *Daten deutscher Dichtung; Chronologischer Abriss der deutschen Literaturgeschichte von den Anfängen bis zur Gegenwart* (3. Auflage; Köln-Berlin: Kiepenheuer & Witsch, 1953) provides a brief literary history of various periods, biographical sketches of the most important authors, as well as a résumé for each title listed. Finally, the *Deutsches Titelbuch; Ein Hilfsmittel zum Nachweis von Verfassern deutscher Literaturwerke* (2. Auflage; Berlin: Haude & Spenersche Verlagsbuchhandlung, 1965), by Max Schneider, supplies a key to the authors and dates of poems, from the first line beginnings.

Minnesinger material is indexed in Robert W. Linker's *The Music of the Minnesinger and Early Meistersinger* (Chapel Hill: University of North Carolina Press, [1962]). Organization is principally by composer, with reference to editions, where available. *A Bibliography of Meistergesang* ([Bloomington: Indiana University, 1936]), by Archer Taylor and Frances H. Ellis, published as *Indiana University Studies,* volume 23, presents mostly criticism, but *Lieder* are listed in the section entitled "Meisterlieder Available in Modern Editions."

In the area of the German Church song, Albert F. W. Fischer's *Kirchenlieder-Lexikon; Hymnologisch-literarische Nachweisungen über ca.4500 der wichtigsten und verbreitesten Kirchenlieder aller Zeiten in alphabetischer Folge nebst einer Übersicht der Liederdichter* (2 vols.; Gotha: [privately printed], 1878-79) is a listing by first lines leading to a full text source.[6] Philipp Wackernagel's *Bibliographie zur Geschichte des deutschen Kirchenliedes im XVI. Jahrhundert* (Frankfurt am Main: Heyder und Zimmer, 1855) is a delineation of editions of the German Church song of the sixteenth century, with bibliographical details.

As we turn to the collections themselves, we should mention first Ludwig Achim von Arnim and Clemens Brentano's *Des Knaben Wunderhorn; Alte deutsche Lieder* (3 vols.; Heidelberg: Mohr u. Zimmer, 1806-8), which has been the source of many texts set by nineteenth- and twentieth-century composers. Following chronologically are Friedrich Heinrich von der Hagen and Johann Gustav Büsching, *Deutsche Gedichte des Mittelalters* (2 vols.; Berlin: Realschulbuchhandlung, [1808-25]); *Neudruck deutscher Litteraturwerke des XVI. und XVII. Jahrhunderts* (325 vols.; Halle: Niemeyer, 1876-1958), also available in a *Neue Folge* (Tübingen: Niemeyer, 1961-); Joseph Kürschner's *Deutsche National-Litteratur; Historische kritische Ausgabe* (163 vols., plus an index volume; Stuttgart: Union Deutsche Verlagsgesellschaft, 1882-98); Karl Victor Müllenhoff and W. Scherer, *Denkmäler deutscher Poesie und Prosa aus dem VIII.-XII. Jahrhundert* (2 vols., 3. Ausgabe; Berlin: Weidmannsche Buchhandlung, 1892); *Deutsche Texte des Mittelalters* (Berlin: Weidmann, 1904-), of which a volume is *Die Gedichte des Michel Beheim; Germanistische Handbibliothek* (Halle: Buchhandlung des Waisenhauses, 1912-), containing Walther von der Vogelweide and Wolfram von Eschenbach; *Deutsche Literatur; Sammlung literarischer Kunst- und Kulturdenkmäler in Entwicklungsreihen* (Leipzig: Reclam, 1928-), of which series 2 is *Geistliche Dichtung des Mittelalters*; Ernst Bertram, August Langen, and Friedrich von der Leyen, *Das Buch deutscher Dichtung* (Leipzig: Insel, 1939-); *Althochdeutsche und Mittelhochdeutsche Epik und Lyrik* (Darmstadt: Wissenschaftliche Buchgesellschaft, 1967-), containing Hartmann von Aue and Gottfried von Strassburg; and Walther Killy's *Die deutsche Literatur; Texte und Zeugnisse* (2. Auflage; München: Beck'sche Verlagsbuchhandlung, 1968-), of which volume 3 is *Das Zeitalter des Barock,* by Albert Schöne.

Smaller collections of early material are three by Karl Bartsch, *Mitteldeutsche Gedichte* (Stuttgart: Litterarischer Verein, 1860); *Beiträge zur Quellenkunde der altdeutschen Literatur* (Strassburg: Trübner, 1886), containing poems with critical commentary; and *Deutsche Liederdichter des zwölften bis vierzehnten Jahrhunderts; Eine Auswahl* (4. Auflage; Berlin: Behr, 1901). Other contributions are Friedrich Wilhelm and Richard Newald, *Poetische Fragmente des 12. und 13.*

---

[6] A musical complement to this title is the important publication by Johannes Zahn, *Die Melodien der deutschen evangelischen Kirchenlieder, aus den Quellen geschöpft und mitgeteilt* (6 vols.; Gütersloh: Bertelsmann, 1889-93).

*Jahrhunderts* (Heidelberg, Winter, 1928), Friedrich von der Leyen, *Deutsche Dichtung des Mittelalters* ([Frankfurt am Main] : Insel, [1962]), Margaret F. Richey, *Medieval German Lyrics* (Edinburgh: Oliver & Boyd, [1964]), Max Wehrli, *Deutsche Barocklyrik* (4. Auflage; Basel: Schwabe, [1967]), Wehrli's *Deutsche Lyrik des Mittelalters* (Zürich: [Manesse Verlag], 1969), Edgar Hederer, *Deutsche Dichtungen des Barock* (München: Hanser, [no date]), and Adalbert Elschenbroich, *Deutsche Dichtung im 18. Jahrhundert* (München: Hanser, [no date]).

Among those titles which contribute folk or popular material is Joseph Görres, *Altdeutsche Volks- und Meisterlieder aus den Handschriften der Heidelberger Bibliothek* (Frankfurt am Main: Wilmans, 1817), which also contains Meistersinger poetry. Further collections in this vein are Friedrich Karl Freiherr von Erlach, *Die Volkslieder der Deutschen; Eine vollständige Sammlung der vorzüglichen deutschen Volkslieder von der Mitte des fünfzehnten bis in die erste Hälfte des neunzehnten Jahrhunderts* (5 vols.; Mannheim: Hoff, 1834-36); Wilhelm Bernhardi, *Allgemeines deutsches Lieder-Lexikon. oder vollständige Sammlung aller bekannten deutschen Lieder und Volksgesänge in alphabetischer Folge* (4 vols.; Leipzig: [privately printed], 1844), with a broad subject index in volume 4; A. H. Hoffmann von Fallersleben, *Die deutschen Gesellschaftslieder des 16. und 17. Jahrhunderts* (2 vols.; Leipzig: Engelmann, 1860); and two compilations by Rochus, Freiherr von Liliencron, *Die historischen Volkslieder der Deutschen vom 13. bis 16. Jahrhunderts* (5 vols.; Leipzig: Vogel, 1865-69) and *Deutsches Leben im Volkslied um 1530* (Berlin and Stuttgart: Spemann, 1855).

The monumental collection of minnesinger verse is Friedrich Heinrich von der Hagen, *Minnesinger; Deutsche Liederdichter des zwölften, dreizehnten und vierzehnten Jahrhunderts, aus allen bekannten Handschriften und früheren Drucken gesammelt und berichtigt, mit den Lesarten derselben, Geschichte des Lebens der Dichter und ihrer Werke, Sangweisen der Lieder, Reimverzeichnis der Anfänge und Abbildungen sämmtlicher Hs.* (5 vols.; Leipzig: Barth, 1838-48). Smaller collections are Karl Friedrich Bartsch, *Die Schweizer Minnesänger* (Frauenfeld: Huber, 1886); Friedrich Pfaff, *Der Minnesang des 12. bis 14. Jahrhunderts* (Stuttgart: Union Deutsche Verlagsgesellschaft, [1890]); Karl Lachmann and Moritz Haupt, *Des Minnesangs Frühling,* edited by Friedrich Vogt (30. Auflage; Leipzig: Hirzel, 1950); Max Wehrli, *Minnesang von Kürenberger bis Wolfram* (2. Auflage; Bern: Francke, [1950]); Carl von Kraus, *Deutsche Liederdichter des 13. Jahrhunderts* (2 vols.; Tübingen: Niemeyer, 1952-58); and Barbara A. G. Seagrave and Wesley Thomas, *The Songs of the Minnesingers* (Urbana: University of Illinois Press, 1966).

In the area of the German Church song, Joseph Kehrein's *Kirchen- und religiöse Lieder aus dem zwölften bis fünfzehnten Jahrhundert* (Paderborn: Schoeningh, 1853) presents Latin and German, with a "Wörterbuch" for German in the back of the volume. Further compilations are the same author's *Katholische Kirchenlieder; Hymnen, Psalmen aus den ältesten deutschen gedruckten Gesang- und Gebetbüchern* (4 vols.; Würzburg: Stahel'sch Buchhandlung, 1859-65), Philipp Wackernagel, *Das deutsche Kirchenlied von der ältesten Zeit bis zu Anfang des XVII. Jahrhunderts; Mit Berücksichtigung der deutschen kirchlichen Liederdichtung im weiteren Sinn und der lateinischen von Hilarius bis Georg Fabricius und Wolfgang Ammonius* (5 vols.; Leipzig: Teubner, 1864-77), and Albert F. W. Fischer and Wilhelm Tümpel, *Das deutsche evangelische Kirchenlied des 17. Jahrhunderts* (6 vols.; Gütersloh, Bertelsmann, 1904-16).

Franz Joseph Mone has contributed two significant collections of early drama. These are *Altdeutsche Schauspiele* (Quedlinberg and Leipzig: Basse, 1841) and *Schauspiele des Mittelalters* (Karlsruhe: Macklot, 1846). Two further compilations are by Richard Froning, *Das Drama des Mittelalters* (3 vols.; Stuttgart: Union Deutsche Verlagsgesellschaft, [1891-92]) and *Das Drama der Reformationszeit* (Stuttgart: Union Deutsche Verlagsgesellschaft, 1895).

## French Texts

In Chapter VII mention has already been made of D. C. Cabeen's comprehensive *Critical Bibliography of French Literature.* Further bibliographical aid may be secured through Robert Bossuat, *Manuel bibliographique de la littérature française du moyen âge* (with supplements of 1955 and 1961; Melun: Libraries d'Argences, 1951); René Rancoeur, *Bibliographie de la littérature française du moyen âge à nos jours* (Paris: Colin, 1953-); the *Dictionnaire des lettres françaises* (Paris: [various publishers], 1939-), under the general editorship of Georges Grente, but with a volume by Robert Bossuat, Louis Pichard, and Guy Raynaud de Lage entitled *Le Moyen âge*; and Nico H. J. van den Boogaard, *Rondeaux et refrains du XIIe siècle au début du XIVe* (Paris: Klincksiek, 1969).

The primary basic bibliography of medieval French poetic literature is Gaston Raynaud's *Bibliographie des chansonniers français des XIIIe et XIVe siècles* (2 vols.; Paris: Vieweg, 1884). Volume 1 analyzes the manuscripts in the order of the library holding them, while volume 2 presents two valuable indexes, a "Liste des chansons classées par ordre alphabétique des rimes," and a "Liste alphabétique des auteurs." A re-working of the Raynaud publication is Hans Spanke's *G. Raynaud's Bibliographie des altfranzösischen Liedes, neu bearbeitet und ergänzt* (Leiden: Bill, 1955). Alfred Jeanroy has supplied two further volumes on this subject, *Bibliographie sommaire des chansonniers provençaux (manuscrits et éditions)* (Paris: Champion, 1916) and *Bibliographie sommaire des chansonniers français du moyen âge (manuscrits et éditions)* (Paris: Champion, 1918). The latter small volume provides a brief description of the manuscripts,

with references to Raynaud or other fuller accounts. Mention should further be made of the bibliographical treatments of J. Brackelmann, *Les plus anciens chansonniers français* (Marburg: Elwert, 1896), Alfred Pillet and Henry Carstens, *Bibliographie der Troubadours* (Halle: Niemeyer, 1933), and Jean Sonet, *Répertoire d'incipit de prières en ancien français* (Genève: Droz, 1956). Sonet has drawn from both manuscript and printed collections.

Somewhat later poetic literature is covered in Artur I. E. Långfors and Paul Meyer, *Les Incipits des poèmes français antérieures au XVIᵉ siècle; Répertoire bibliographique* (Paris: Champion, [1917]), which excludes lyric poetry and the *chanson de geste* except for that not covered by Raynaud, and in two works by Frédéric Lachèvre, *Bibliographie des recueils collectifs de poésies publiés de 1597 à 1700* (5 vols.; Paris: Leclerc, 1901-22) and *Bibliographie des recueils collectifs de poésies du XVIᵉ siècle* (Paris: Champion, 1922).

Turning to the collections themselves, we find two prior to the nineteenth century, *Le Jardin de plaisance et fleur de rhétorique* (2 vols.; Paris: Firmin-Didot, 1924), first published in 1501 and of considerable importance for music research, and the *Almanach des muses* (69 vols.; Paris: Delalain, 1766-93). Following chronologically are *Les poètes françois depuis le XIIᵉ siècle jusqu'à Malherbe* (6 vols.; Paris: Crapelet, 1824); Anatole de Courde de Montaiglon, *Recueil de poésies françoises des XVᵉ et XVIᵉ siècles* (13 vols.; Paris: Jannet, 1855-78); the publications of the *Société des anciens textes français* (Paris: Firmin-Didot, 1876-), a comprehensive collection containing among its volumes the *Oeuvres de Guillaume Machaut;* the *Recueil des motets français des XIIᵉ et XIIIᵉ siècles* (2 vols.; Paris: Vieweg, 1881-83), by Gaston Raynaud and Henri Lavoix; and the *Bibliothèque meridionale* (Toulouse: Privat, 1888-), sponsored by the University of Toulouse and containing, for example, Alfred Jeanroy's *Les joies du gai savoir; Recueil de poésies couronnées par le consistoire de la gaie science (1324-1484).* From the twentieth century one has Fernand Fleuret and Louis Perceau, *Les satires françaises du XVIIᵉ siècle* (2 vols.; Paris: Garnier, 1923), Artur I. E. Långfors, A. Jeanroy, and L. Brandin, *Recueil général des jeuxpartis français* (2 vols.; Paris: Champion, 1926), *Grands poètes français; Le seizième siècle* (2 vols.; Lausanne: Kaeser, 1947), Jean Rousset, *Anthologie de la poésie baroque française* (2 vols.; Paris: Colin, 1961), Alan M. Boase, *The Poetry of France* (London: Methuen, 1964-), Maurice Allem, *Anthologie poétique française; XVIᵉ siècle* (Paris: Garnier-Flammerion, 1965-), and the *Anthologie de la poésie française* (5 vols.; Montreal: Valiquette, [no date]).

Smaller collections with chronological orientation are Wilhelm Wackernagel, *Altfranzoesische Lieder und Leiche aus Handschriften zu Bern und Neuenburg* (Basel: Schweighauser, 1846); Edélestand P. Du Méril, *Poésies inédites du moyen âge* (Paris: Franck, 1854); Antoine J. V. Le Roux de Lincy, *Le livre des proverbes français* (2. éd.; Paris: Delahays, 1859); Karl F. Bartsch, *Romances et pastourelles françaises des XIIᵉ et XIIIᵉ siècles; Altfranzösische Romanzen und*

*Pastourellen* (Leipzig: Vogel, 1870), drawn from twenty-six manuscripts; K. F.
Bartsch and A. Hornung, *La langue et la littérature françaises depuis le IX^ème
siècle jusqu'au XIV^ème siecle* (Paris: Maisonneuve & Leclerc, 1887); and Fritz
Noack, *Der Strophenausgang in seinen Verhältnis zum Refrain und Strophen-
grundstock in der altfranzösischen Lyrik* (Marburg: Elwert, 1899), including
sixty-six texts. Continuing to the middle of our own century we have Alfred
Jeanroy, *Chansons jeux parties et refrains inédits* (Toulouse and Paris: Privat,
1902); Ernest Langlois, *Recueil d'arts de seconde rhétorique* (Paris: [privately
printed], 1902); Mayer A. M. Schwob, *Le parnasse satyrique du quinzième siècle;
Anthologie de pièces libres* (Paris: Welter, 1905); Edw. Järnström, *Recueil de
chansons pieuses du XIII^e siècle* (Helsinki: Suomalaison Tiedeakatemian
Toimituksia, 1910); Elisabeth Heldt, *Französische Virelais aus dem 15. Jahrh.*
(Halle: Niemeyer, 1916); Karl F. Bartsch, *Chrestomathie de l'ancien français
(VIII^e-XV^e siècles)* (12. éd.; Leipzig: Vogel, 1920), containing poems by Blondel
de Nesle, Gace Brulé, and Adam de la Halle, among others; Alfred Jeanroy and
A. Langfors, *Chansons satiriques et bachiques du XIII^e siècle* (Paris: Champion,
1921), with orientation according to such subjects as "Contre le siècle," or
"Contre l'amour"; Jeanroy's *Poèmes et récits de la vieille France* (Paris: Boccard,
1923); André Dumas, *Anthologie des poètes français du XVII^e siècle* (Paris:
Delagrave, 1933), with poems, for example, by Benserade and La Fontaine;
Henry Poulaille, *La Fleur des chansons d'amour du XVI^e siècle* (Paris: Grasset,
[1943]); Thierry Maulnier, *Poésie du XVII^ème siècle* (Paris: La Table Ronde,
1945); and Ferdinand Duviard, *Anthologie de poètes français (XVII^e siècle)*
(Paris: Larousse, 1947). From 1950 onward collections of importance are
Albert M. Schmidt, *Poètes du XVI^e siècle* ([Paris]: Gallimard, 1953), including
Clément Marot among others; I. M. Cluzel and L. Pressouyre, *Les origines de la
pośie lyrique d'oïl et les premiers trouvères; Textes* (Paris: Nizet, 1962); Victor
Graham, *Sixteenth-Century French Poetry* ([Toronto]: University of Toronto
Press, [c1964]); Pierre Groult, V. Emont, and G. Muraille, *Anthologie de la
Littérature française du moyen âge des origines à la fin du XIII^e siècle* (2 vols.,
3. éd.; Gembloux: Duculot, 1964), with some anonymous poems; Alfred
Jeanroy, *Les origines de la poésie lyrique en France au moyen âge* (4. éd.; Paris:
Champion, 1965), largely discussion, but with twenty-nine poems; Guillaume
Picot, *La poésie lyrique au moyen âge* (2 vols.; Paris: Larousse, 1965); Albert
Henry, *Chrestomathie de la littérature en ancien français* (2 vols.; Berne: Francke,
1965); Odette de Mourges, *An Anthology of French Seventeenth-Century Lyric
Poetry* (London: Oxford University Press, 1966); Floyd Gray, *Anthologie de la
poésie française du XVI^e siècle* (New York: Appleton-Century-Crofts, 1967);
Nigel Wilkins, *One Hundred Ballades, Rondeaux, and Virelais from the Late Middle
Ages* (Cambridge: University Press, 1969), which includes a small musical appendix;
Jean Charles Payen, *Les moyen âge, I; Des origines à 1300* (Paris: Arthaud, 1970);
and Daniel Poirion, *Le moyen âge, II; 1300-1480* (Paris: Arthaud, 1971).

Some collections demonstrating regional poetic art are Louis F. Du Bois, *Vaux-de-Vire d'Olivier Basselin, poëte normand de la fin du XIVᵉ siècle; Suivis d'un choix d'anciens vaux-de-vire, de Bacchanales et de chansons, poésies normandes soit inédites, soit devenues excessivement rares* (Caen: Poisson, 1821); Karl Bartsch, *Denkmäler der provenzalischer Litteratur* (Stuttgart: Litterarischer Verein, 1856), with an index of names which appear in the poems; Prosper Tarbé, *Collections des poètes champenois antérieurs au XVIᵉ siècle* (24 vols.; [place varies: various publishers], 1847–64); Armand Gasté, *Chansons normandes du XVᵉ siècle, publiées pour la premier fois sur les mss de Bayeux et de Vire* (Caen: Le Gost-Clerisse, 1866); Paul Meyer, *Recueil d'anciens textes bas-latines, provençaux et français* (Paris: Vieweg, 1877); and Jean F. Bladé, *Poésies populaires de la Gascogne* (3 vols.; Paris: Maisonneuve & Larose, [c.1881]). Karl Bartsch's *Chrestomathie provençale* (6. éd.; Marburg: Elwert, 1904) includes a large glossary as well as a "Tableau sommaire des flexions provençales," and some texts are included in Amédée G. Pagès' *La poésie française en Catalogne du XIIIᵉ siècle à la fin du XVᵉ* (Toulouse: Privat, 1936).

Troubadour poetry may be found in François J. M. Raynouard's *Choix des poésies originales des troubadours* (6 vols.; Paris: Didot, 1816–21), with a full historical discussion and tabular comparisons. Other works from the nineteenth century containing troubadour, trouvère or associated verse are Achille Jubinal, *Jongleurs et trouvères, ou choix des saluts, épitres, rêveries et autres pièces légères des XIIIᵉ et XIVᵉ siècles* (Paris: Merklein, 1835) and Friedrich C. Diez, *Die Poesie der Troubadours* (2. Auflage; Leipzig: Barth, 1883). From our own century we have Alfred Jeanroy, *Jongleurs et troubadours gascons des XIIᵉ et XIIIᵉ siècles* (Paris: Champion, 1923); Olga Dobiache-Rojdestventsky, *Les Poésies lyrique des goliards* (Paris: Rieder, 1931); Alfred Jeanroy, *La poésie lyrique des troubadours* (2 vols.; Toulouse: Privat, 1934); Robert S. Briffault, *The Troubadours,* edited by Lawrence F. Koons (Bloomington: Indiana University Press, 1965), containing troubadour melodies; René Nelli and René Lavaud, *Les Troubadours* (2 vols.; Paris: Desclée De Brouwer, 1960–66), with facing translations into modern French; Pierre Bec, *Nouvelle anthologie de la lyrique occitane du moyen âge* (Avignon: Aubanel, 1970); and Alan R. Press, *Anthology of Troubadour Lyric Poetry* (Austin: University of Texas Press, 1971), with facing translation into English.

Popular or historical poetry is included in Oskar L. B. Wolff, *Altfranzösische Volkslieder* (Leipzig: Fleischer, 1831); Antoine J. V. Le Roux de Lincy, *Recueil de chants historiques français depuis le XIIᵉ jusqu'au XVIIIᵉ siècle* (2 vols.; Paris: Gosselin, 1841); Charles Nisard, *Des chansons populaires* (2 vols.; Paris: Dentu, 1867), with substantial critical discussion; Anatole de Courde de Montaiglon, *Recueil général et complet des fabliaux des XIIIᵉ et XIVᵉ siècles, imprimés ou inédits* (6 vols.; Paris: Libraries des Bibliophiles, 1872–90); Emile

Raunié, *Chansonnier historique du XVIIIe siècle* (10 vols.; Paris: Quantin,
1879-84), which proceeds chronologically by year; and Jean B. T. Weckerlin,
*L'ancienne chanson populaire en France (16e et 17e siècles)* (Paris: Garnier,
1887), with a "Bibliographie chansonnière." Carols may be found in Henry
Poulaille, *La grande et belle Bible des noëls anciens* (Paris: Michel, [1942-51])
and in the same author's *Bible des noëls anciens des origines au seizième siècle*
(éd. nouvelle; [Paris: Club des Editeurs, 1958]).

French dramatic production is contained in Claude B. Petitot, *Répertoire du
théatre français* (23 vols., together with the supplement of eight volumes
published Paris, Foucault, 1819; Paris: Didot, 1803-4). Three large compilations
by Pierre M. M. Lepeintre-Desroches are *Suite du répertoire du théatre français*
(81 vols.; Paris: Dabo, 1822-23), *Fin du répertoire du théatre français* (44 vols.;
Paris: Dabo, 1824), and *Bibliothèque dramatique, ou Répertoire universal du
théatre français* (36 vols.; Paris: [various publishers], 1824-25). Further
collections of drama are *Pièces de théatre* (192 vols.; Bruxelles: [various
publishers], 1826-55), containing a good many opera librettos; *Collection des
théâtres français* (5 series; Senlis: Tremblay, 1829); Antoine J. V. Le Roux de
Lincy and Francisque Michel, *Recueil de farces, moralités et sermons joyeaux*
(3 vols.; Paris: Téchener, 1837-41); Emmanuel L. N. Viollet-Le-Duc, *Ancien
théatre français* (10 vols.; Paris: Jannet, 1854-57); Victor Fournel, *Les
contemporains de Molière* (3 vols.; Paris: Didot, 1863-75); Paul Lacroix, *Ballets
et mascarades de cour, de Henri III à Louis XIV (1581-1652)* (6 vols.; Turin:
Gay, 1868-70); Edouard Fournier, *Le théatre français au XVIe et au XVIIe
siècle* (Paris: Corbeil, 1871); Fournier's *Le théatre français avant la Renaissance,
1450-1550* (Paris: Laplace, Sanchez, 1872), containing "mystères, moralités, et
farces"; the same author's *Le théâtre français au XVIe et au XVIIe siècle, ou
Choix des comédies les plus remarquables, antérieures à Molière* (Paris: Laplace,
Sanchez, [1874]), and *Petites comédies rares et curieuses du XVIIe siècle*
(2 vols.; Paris: Quantin, 1884); and Alfred Jeanroy and H. Teulié, *Mystères
provencaux du quinzième siècle* (Toulouse: Privat, 1893). From our own
century we have Alfred Jeanroy, *Le théâtre religieux en France du XIe au XIIIe
siècles* (Paris: Boccard, 1924) and Gustave Cohen, *Recueil de farces françaises
inédites du XVe siècle* (Cambridge, Mass.: Mediaeval Academy of America,
1949), with analytical indexes and glossary.


## Italian Texts

Mazzoni's *Avviamento allo studio critico delle lettere italiane* has been mentioned
in Chapter VII. Further recent works of bibliographical importance are Lanfranco
Caretti, *Avviamento allo studio della letteratura italiana* (Firenze: La Nuova Italia,
1953), which contains general sections as well as those on individual poets; Walter

Binni and Riccardo Scrivano, *Introduzione ai problemi critici della letteratura italiana* (Messina-Firenze: D'anna, [1967]), which presents analyses of literary series; Mario Puppo's *Manuale critico-bibliografico per lo studio della letteratura italiana* (11. ed.; Torino: Società Editrice Internazionale, 1971); and Giorgio Petrocchi and Ferruccio Ulivi, *Stile e critica; Avviamento alla studio della letteratura italiana* (Bari: Adriatica, 1968).

Bibliographies or indexes of the verse itself are Gaetano Melzi, *Bibliografia dei romanzi e poemi cavallereschi italiani* (2. ed.; Milano: Tosi, 1838), Giulio Gnaccarini, *Indice delle antiche rime volgari a stampa che fanno v. 98-99 parte della biblioteca Carducci* (2 vols.; Bologna: Dall'Acqua, 1909), and A. Tenneroni, *Inizi di antiche poesie italiane religiose e morali* (Firenze: Olschki, 1909). The subject of the *lauda* is covered in G. Fabris, *Il più antico laudario veneto, con la bibliografia delle laude* (Vicenza: Giuseppe, 1907) and in Gennaro M. Monti, *Bibliographia delle Laude* (Firenze: Olschki, 1925).

The eighteenth century produced a large collection of earlier poetic material of considerable importance to musical research. This is *Tutti i trionfi, carri, mascherate, o canti carnascialeschi andati per Firenze dal tempo del Magnifico Lorenzo de' Medici, fino al anno 1559* (2 vols., 2. ed.; [Lucca: Benedini], 1750). Significant nineteenth-century collections are G. H. A. Wagner, *Il Parnasso italiano* (2 vols.; Lipsia: Fleischer, 1826-33), containing Dante, Ariosto, Tasso, and others; *Raccolta dei più celebri poemi eroi-comici italiani* (3 vols.; Firenze: Parenti, 1841-42); *Biblioteca Nazionale* (Firenze: Le Monnier, 1843-); Francesco Trucchi, *Poesie italiane inedite di dugento autori, dall'origine della lingua in fino al secolo decimosettimo* (4 vols.; Prato: Guasti, 1846-47); *Raccolta di opere inedite o rare* (Firenze: Sansoni, 1880-), including A. Bartoli's *Scenari inediti della commedia dell'arte;* and *Biblioteca di classici italiani* (Firenze: Sansoni, 1885-). From the twentieth century we have the *Classici italiani* (in two series; Torino: UTET, 1911-); the large *Scrittori d'Italia* (Bari: Laterza, 1912-), of which a volume is the fourteenth-century *Il libro delle rime* by Franco Sacchetti in the edition of Alberto Chiari; Giuseppe Prezzolini, *I maggiori autori della letteratura italiana* (6 vols.; Milano: Mondadori, 1925-29); *Autori classici e documenti di lingua* (Firenze: Sansoni, 1926-); *Collezione di opere inedite o rare de' primi tre secoli della lingua* (Bologna: Romagnoli-Dall'Acqua, 1926-); *Le più belle pagine degli Scrittori italiani* (Milano: Treves, 1933-); the *Classici Mondadori* (Milano: Mondadori, 1935), specializing in "complete works"; the *Classici Rizzoli* (in two series; Milano: Rizzoli, 1935-), with a volume by C. Calcaterra entitled *Lirici del Seicento e dell'Arcadia;* Giuseppe Lipparini, *Le pagine della letteratura italiana* (20 vols.; Milano: Signorelli, 1935-38); Lipparini's *I grandi autori della letteratura italiana* (3 vols.; Milano: Signorelli, 1937); Giuseppe Zoppi, *Antologia della letteratura italiana* (Verona: Mondadori, 1939-); Lipparini's *Esempi di letteratura italiana* (4 vols.; Milano: Signorelli, 1943-44); Luigi Russo's *I classici italiani* (6 vols.; Firenze: Sansoni, 1951); the *Parnaso italiano* (Torino: Einaudi, 1954-); *La letteratura italiana, Storia e testi* (Milano: Ricciardi, 1956); *Biblioteca di classici italiani* (Milano: Feltrinelli, 1960-); *Antologia della letteratura italiana* (3 vols.; Torino: Società Editrice Internazionale, 1960-62); and the *Classici italiani* (Bologna: Zanichelli, 1966-).

Anthologies of lyrics devoted to periods which are volumes of large collections are listed in the Binni and Scrivano volume mentioned above. It would seem appropriate, however, to mention some of the more important titles here. Beginning with thirteenth-century verse we have Eugenia Levi, *Lirica italiana antica* (Florence: Olschki, 1905), Giosuè Carducci, *Antica lirica italiana (canzonette, canzoni, sonetti dei secoli XIII-XV)* (Firenze: Sansoni, 1907), Arthur J. Butler, *The Forerunners of Dante; A Selection of Italian Poetry before 1300* (Oxford: Clarendon Press, 1910), Guido Zaccagnini and Amos Parducci, *Rimatori siculo-toscani del dugento* (Bari: Laterza, 1915), Luigi di Benedetto, *Poemetti allegorico-didattici del secolo XIII* (Bari: Laterza, 1941), Giuseppe Petronio, *Poemetti del Duecento* ([Torino] : UTET, [1951]), Carlo Salinari, *La poesia lirica del Duecento* ([Torino] : UTET, [1951]), Carlo Muscetta, *Poesia del Duecento e del Trecento* (Torino: Einaudi, 1956), Gianfranco Contini, *Poeti del Duecento* (2 vols.; Milano: Ricciardi, [1960]), and Maria P. La Valva, *Rime italiane del Duecento* (Tübingen: Niemeyer, 1965). The "dolce stil nuovo" is represented in Luigi di Benedetto, *Rimatori del dolce stil novo* (Bari: Laterza, 1939), containing Guinizelli, Cavalcanti, Cino da Pistoia, and others; Vittore Branca, *Rimatori del dolce stil novo* (Genova: Editrice Dante Alighieri, 1941); Ernesto Monaci, *Crestomazia italiana dei primi secoli,* edited by F. Arese (nuova ed.; Roma: Società Editrice Dante Alighieri, 1955); and Mario Marti, *Poeti del Dolce Stil Nuovo* ([Firenze] : Le Monnier, [1969]). Trecento verse may be found in Giosuè Carducci, *Rime di M. Cino da Pistoia e d'altri del secolo XIV* (Firenze: Barbéra, 1862), Natalino Sapegno, *Poeti minori del Trecento* (Milano: Ricciardi, [1952]), Mario Marti, *Poeti giocosi del tempo di Dante* (Milano: Rizzoli, [1956]), and Giuseppe G. Ferroro, *Poemi cavallereschi del Trecento* ([Torino] : UTET, [1965]). Verse of the two following centuries is found in Carlo Muscetta and Daniele Ponchiroli, *Poesia del Quattrocento e del Cinquencento* ([Torino] : Einaudi, 1959). Collections of sixteenth-century verse are *Lirici del secolo XVI* (Milano: Sonzogno, 1879), containing poetic material by Pietro Bembo, Lodovico Ariosto, Michelangelo Buonarroti, and others; Luigi Baldacci, *Lirici del cinquecento* ([Firenze] : Salani, [1957]); and Giacinto Spagnoletti, *Il petrarchismo* ([Milano] : Garzanti, [1959]). Collections of seventeenth-century poems are Benedetto Croce, *Lirici marinisti* (Bari: Laterza, 1910); Ettore Allodoli, *Le più belle pagine dei poeti burleschi del Seicento* (Milano: Treves, 1925), containing humorous and parodic lyrics; Giovanni Getto, *Marino e i marinisti, opere scelte* (2 vols.; Torino: UTET, 1954); and Carlo Muscetta's and Pier Paolo Ferrante's *Poesia del Seicento* (2 vols.; [Torino] : Einaudi, [1964]). Finally, poetry from the eighteenth century is represented in

Giosuè Carducci's *Lirici del secolo XVIII* (Firenze: Barbèra, 1871) and *Poeti erotici del secolo XVIII* (Firenze: Barbèra, 1868), Severino Ferrari's *Antologia della lirica moderna* (Bologna: Zanichelli, 1931), Mario Sansone's *Favolisti del Settecento* (Firenze: Sansoni, [1943]), Bruno Maier's *Lirici del Settecento* (Milano: Ricciardi, [1959]), and Carlo Muscetta's and M. R. Massei's *Poesia del Settecento* (Torino: Einaudi, 1967).

A very interesting collection of Sicilian poetry is found in *Italienische Lieder des Hohenstaufischen Hofes in Sicilien* (Stuttgart: Literarischer Verein, 1843), containing verse of the Emperor Frederick II and others. Further Sicilian collections are Ettore Li Gotti, *Volgare nostro siculo; Crestomazia dei testi in antico siciliano del secolo XIV* (Firenze: La Nuova Italia, [1954]), and two works edited by Bruno Panvini, *La scuola poetica siciliana* (2 vols.; Firenze: Olschki, 1957-58) and *Le rime della scuola siciliana* (Firenze: Olschki, 1962-). Two compilations of Venetian poetry are Raffaelo Barbiera, *Poesie veneziane* (Firenze: Barbèra, 1886) and Manlio T. Dazzi, *Il fiore della lirica veneziana* (2 vols.; Venezia: Pozza, 1966).

Two significant publications of *canti carnascialeschi*, both by Charles S. Singleton, are *Canti carnscialeschi del Rinascimento* (Bari: Laterza, 1936), part of the series *Scrittori d'Italia*, mentioned above, and *Nuovi canti carnscialeschi del Rinascimento* (Modena: Soc. Tip. Modenese, 1940). Sonnets have been collected by August Buck, in *Italienische Sonette (13.-17. Jahrhundert) in Auswahl* (Tübingen: Niemeyer, 1954), and by Giovanni Arcidiacono, in *Il sonetto italiano dalle origini ai nostri giorni* (Firenze: Il Fauno, [1962]). Other genre collections are Giosuè Carducci, *Cacce in rima dei secoli XIV e XV* (Bologna: Zanichelli, 1896), Carducci's *Cantilene e ballate, strambotti e madrigali nei secoli XIII e XIV* (Sesto S. Giovanni: Madella, 1912), and Gustavo Galletti, *Laude spirituali di Feo Belcari, di Lorenzo de' Medici, di Francesco d'Albizzo, di Castellano Castellani e di altri* (Firenze: Cecchi, 1863).

Compilations of popular poetry are by Antonio Casetti, *Canti populari delle provincie meridionali* (2 vols.; Roma: Loescher, 1871-72), Alessandro d'Ancona, *Venti canti popolari siciliani* (Livorno: [privately printed], 1877), Giosuè Carducci, *La poesia barbara nei secoli XV e XVI* (Bologna: Zanichelli, 1881), and Alessandro Ancona, *Poemetti popolari italiani* (Bologna: Zanichelli, 1889). Ancona's *La poesia popolare italiana* (2. ed.; Livorno: Giusti, 1906) is valuable for its "Indicazione bibliografica delle raccolte di poesia popolari e di altre opere più spesso citate nel corso del lavoro" and its table of fourteenth-century poems used as *laude*. Two further collections of popular verse are Erhard Lommatzsch, *Beiträge zur älteren italienischen Volksdichtung; Untersuchungen und Texte* (3 vols.; Berlin: Akademie-Verlag, 1950-51) and Fernando Figurelli, *La poesia comico-giocosa dei primi due secoli* (Napoli: Pironti, [1960]).

Compilations of Italian drama are *Teatro italiano, o sia scelta di tragedia per uso della scena* (3 vols.; Verona: Vallarsi, 1723-25), containing Trissino, Rucellai,

Giustiniano, and other playwrights; *Le Nouveau théâtre italien, ou Recueil général des comédies representées par les Comédies italiens du Roi* (9 vols., nouv. éd.; Paris: Briasson, 1733-50), including some music; *Teatro italiano antico* (10 vols.; Milano: Società Tipografia de' Classici Italiani, 1808-12); *Teatro classico italiano antico e moderno* (Lipsia: Fleischer, 1829); *Teatro tragico italiano* (Firenze: Borghi, 1832); Vincenzo de Bartholomaeis, *Laude drammatiche e rappresentazioni sacre* (3 vols.; Firenze: Le Monnier, 1943); *Teatro italiano* (5 vols.; [Milano]: Nuova Accademia Editrice, [1955-56]); and Alessandro Perosa, *Teatro umanistico* ([Milano]: Nuova Accademia Editrice, 1965). Collections with chronological orientation are Mario Bonfantini, *Le sacre rappresentazioni italiane; Raccolta di testi dal secolo XIII al secolo XVI* ([Milano]: Bompiani, [1942]); Alessandro d'Ancona, *Sacre rappresentazioni dei secoli XIV, XV e XVI* (Firenze: Successori Le Monnier, 1872); Mario Apollonario, *Commedia italiana; Raccolta di commedia da Cielo d'Alcamo a Goldoni* ([Milano]: Bompiani, 1947); Nino Borsellino, *Commedie del Cinquecento* ([Milano]: Feltrinelli, [1962-]); Anton Giulio Bragaglia, *Commedie giocose del Cinquecento* ([Roma]: Colombo, 1946-), containing Ariosto, Cecchi, Aretino, and others; Domenico Coppola, *Sacre rappresentazioni aversane del sec. XVI* (Firenze: Olschki, 1959); Ireneo Sanesi, *Commedie del Cinquecento* (Bari: Laterza, 1912-); Paolo Toschi, *Sacre rappresentazioni toscane dei secoli XV e XVI* (Firenze: Olschki, 1969); Luigi Fassò, *Teatro del Seicento* (Milano: Ricciardi, [1956]); and G. Gasperini, *La tragedia classica dalle origini al Maffei* (Torino: UTET, 1963). A regionally oriented collection is Orio Vergano and Fortunato Rosti, *Teatro milanese* (2 vols.; [Bologna]: Guanda, 1958).

## Spanish Texts

B eyond the Grismer work brought out in Chapter VII, general bibliographies of Spanish literature are James Fitzmaurice-Kelly, *Spanish Bibliography* (London: Oxford University Press, 1925); Antonio Palau y Dulcet, *Manual del librero hispano-americano* (2nd ed.; Barcelona: Palau, 1948-), a very comprehensive bibliography arranged alphabetically by author; Homero Serís, *Manual de bibliografía de la literatura española* (2 vols.; Syracuse: Centro de Estudios Hispanicos, 1948-54); and two works by José Simon Diaz, *Bibliografía de la literatura hispánica* (Madrid: Consejo Superior de Investigaciones Científicas, 1950-), which is detailed, with a subject and index for each volume, and *Manual de bibliografía de la literatura española* (2. ed.; Barcelona: Gil, 1966). Poetic literature is covered in Francisco Marti Grajales, *Ensayo de un diccionario biográfico y bibliográfico de los poetas que florecieron en el reino de Valencia hasta el año 1700* (Madrid: Rivista de Archivos, Bibliotecas y Museos, 1927); Antonio R. Rodriguez Moñino, *Catálogo de los manuscritos poéticos castellanos existentes en la Biblioteca de The Hispanic Society of America (siglos XV, XVI y XVII)* (3 vols.; New York: Hispanic Society of America, 1965-66), of particular interest to Americans; and the same author's *Diccionario bibliográfico de pliegos sueltos poéticos (siglo XVI)* (Madrid: Editorial Castalia, 1970), provided with an "Indice de tonas para cantar y bailes!" In addition, two poetic bibliographies might be mentioned, both with special orientation and both by José Simón Diaz. These are *Impresos del XVI: Poesía* (Madrid: C. S. I. C., 1964), a listing of 273 items beginning with the year 1508, and *Siglos de oro: Indice de justas poéticas* (Madrid: C. S. I. C., 1962), provided with an index of participating authors and of libraries holding these works. Bibliographies of drama are Cayetano Alberto de la Barrera y Leirado, *Catálogo bibliográfico y biográfico del teatro antiguo español* (Madrid: Rivadeneyra, 1860), with coverage to about 1750, and Raymond L. Grismer *Bibliography of the Drama of Spain and Spanish America* (Minneapolis: Burgess-Beckwith, [1966]), provided with an index of proper names.

Turning to the collections themselves, we have three from the nineteenth century. The first in point of time is the *Coleccion de los mejores autores españoles* (60 vols.; Paris: Baudry, 1838-72). This is known as the "Collection Baudry" and includes as volume 20 Tomás Antonio Sánchez' *Coleccion de poesias castellanos anteriores al siglo XV*. Proceeding chronologically we find Marcelino Mendéndez y Pelayo, *Antología de poetas líricos castellanos desde la formación del idioma hasta nuestras días* (13 vols.; Madrid: Viuda de Hernando, 1890-1916) and Pedro Espinosa, *Primera [segunda] parte de las Flores de poetas illustres de España* (2 vols., 2. ed.; Sevilla: Rasco, 1896), the latter containing copious notes. From our century we may mention the *Nueva biblioteca de autores Españoles* (24 vols.; Madrid: Librería Editorial de Bailly-Balliére e Hijos, 1905-17), which contains as a double volume R. Foulché-Delbosc' edition of the *Cancionero Castellano de siglo XV*; the *Antología de poeticas líricas* (2 vols.; Madrid: Tip. de la "Revista de arch., bibl. y museos," 1915); *Biblioteca de autores Españoles* (Madrid: Real Academia Española, 1944, the second edition of a set begun in 1846 by the publisher Rivadeneyra); María Goyri and Ramón Menéndez Pidal, *Romancero tradicional de las lenguas hispánicas* (2 vols.; Madrid: Editorial Gredos, 1957-63), in which the material is organized by genre; Ramón Menéndez Pidal, *Pliegos poéticos Españoles en la Universidad de Praga* (2 vols.; Madrid: [no publisher], 1960); and Arthur Terry, *An Anthology of Spanish Poetry, 1500-1700* (2 vols.; Oxford: Pergamon Press, [1965-68]).

In considering editions devoted to periods we shall progress more or less in chronological order. Prior to the sixteenth century we have Dámaso Alonso, *Poesía de la edad media y poesía de tipo tradicional* (Buenos Aires: Editorial Losada, 1942); Adolfo Bonilla y San Martín, *Antología de poetas de los siglos XIII al XV* (Madrid: Ruiz hermanos, 1917), including plates of music; Simon González, *Poesía medieval* (Madrid: Consejo Superior de Investigaciones Cientificas, 1947); and Felipe Maldonada, *Edad media española: textos escogidos*

110                                    Indexes and Editions of Vocal Texts

(Madrid: Taurus, 1959); *Pliegos poeticos góticos* (6 vols.; Madrid: ["Joyas Bibliográficas"], 1957-61), a facsimile edition of poetic prints of the fifteenth and sixteenth centuries in gothic type; *Colección de algunas poesías castellanas anteriores al siglo XV* (Madrid: Lalama, 1841), which is intended as a continuation of Tomas Antonio Sánchez' *Colección de poesias castellanas anteriores al siglo XV* (4 vols.; Madrid: Sancha, 1779-90); and Ruggieri Scudieri, *Poesia cortese dei secoli XIV e XV nella penisola iberica* (Modena: Società Tipografica Modenese, 1956), boasting a large introduction. The sixteenth century is represented by Pedro Blanco Suárez, *Poetas de los siglos XVI y XVII* (Madrid: Instituto-Escuela, 1923), Adolfo Bonilla y San Martin, *Flores de poetas ilustres de los siglos XVI y XVII* (Madrid: Hermanos, 1917), Rafael Lapesa, *Poetas del siglo XVI; Periodo clásico (1525-1590)* (Barcelona: Rauter, [1947]), and Giovanni Maria Bertini, *Poesia spagnola del seicento* (Torino: Chiantore, 1946). Poetry of the Golden Age is collected in Milton A. Buchanan, *Spanish Poetry of the Golden Age* (Toronto: University of Toronto Press, 1942), an annotated edition of verse from 1400 to 1640; Phyllis D. Tettenhorn, *Spanish Lyrics of the Golden Age* (London: Bell, 1952); and Bruce W. Wardropper, *Spanish Poetry of the Golden Age* (New York: Appleton-Century-Crofts, [1971]). A small anthology of later material is Adolfo Bonilla y San Martín's *Parnaso español de los siglos XVIII y XIX* (Madrid: Hermanos, 1917).

   Turning now from chronological considerations to regional ones we should mention two collections by Manuel Alvar López, *Poesía española dialectal* (Madrid: Alcalá, [1965]), which includes a "Bibliografía fundamental," and *Textos hispánicos dialectales; Antología histórica* (Madrid: Consejo Superior de Investigaciones Cientifícas, 1960), with a large "Vocabulario." Attention has been given to Castilian verse in Juan Nicolás Böhl de Faber, *Floresta de rimas antiguas castellanas* (Hamburgo: Perthes y Besser, 1821), Isidro Gabriel, *Los mejores romances de la lengua castellana* ([Buenos Aires: Fabril, 1961]), Fernando Gutiérrez, *La poesía castellana: Los primitivos* (Barcelona: Jánes, 1950), Rafael Morales, *Los 100 poetas mejores de la lírica castellana; Antología* (Madrid: Giner, [1967]), and Juan José López de Sedano, *Parnaso español; Collección de poesías escogidas de los mas célebres poetas castellanos* (9 vols.; Madrid: Ibarra, 1768-78). Poetry from Sevilla is recorded in *Justas poéticas sevillanas del siglo XVI* (Valencia: Castalia, 1955), which reprints publications of 1531 to 1542, and Alberto Sánchez, *Poesía sevillana en la edad de oro* (Madrid: Editorial Castilla, [1948]), which is prefaced by a study on Fernando de Herrera (1534-1597). Two very specialized regional collections are Henry R. Lang, *Cancioneiro gallego-castelhano; The Extant Galician Poems of the Gallego-Castilian Lyric School (1350-1450)* (New Haven: Yale University Press, 1913-) and Manuel Milá y Fontanals, *Romancerillo catalán* (2. ed.; Barcelona: Verdaguer, 1882).

   Popular poetry may be found in Rafael Albert, *Eglogas y fabulas castellanas* (2 vols.; Buenos Aires: Pleamar, [1944]); Julio Cejador y Frauca, *La verdadera*

*poesía castellana; Floresta de la antigua lírica popular* (5 vols.; Madrid: Tip. de
la "Rev. de arch., bibl. y museos," 1921-24); Margit Frenk Alatorre, *Lírica
hispánica de tipo popular; Edad media y renacimento* (México: [Universidad
Autónoma de México], 1966), including a large bibliography; Enrique Llovet,
*Magia y milagro de la poesía popular* (Madrid: Editora Nacional, 1956); and
Santiago Magariños, *Canciones populares de la edad de oro* ([Barcelona] :
Lauro, 1944). Theatrical verse may be located in Mariano Catalina y Cobo,
*La poesía lírica en el teatro antiguo* (11 vols.; Madrid: [various publishers] ,
1909-14), which includes a "Lista de las obras dramáticas" in each volume,
and Justo Garcia Morales, *Poesías líricas en el teatro español, siglos XIII a XX*
([Madrid] : Aguilar, [ᶜ1950] ).

Special collections of Spanish verse are Manuel Alvar Lopez, *Poemas
hagiográficos de carácter juglaresco* (Madrid: Ediciones Alcala, [1967]); Agustí
Bartra, *Antología poética de la muerte* (México: Editorial Pan-Mexico, [1967]);
Paul Benichou, *Romancero Judeo-Español de Marruecos* (Madrid: Editorial
Castalia, 1968); and Alvar Lopez', *Poesía tradicional de los judios españoles*
(Mexico: Porrua, 1966), which has appended "Illustraciones musicales." Further
collections are Ramón Mendéndez Pidal, *Reliquias de la poesía épica española*
(Madrid: [Espasa-Calpe] , 1951), Eugenio de Ochoa y Ronna, *Tesoro de los
poemas españoles épicos, sagrados, y burlescos* (Paris: Garnier hermanos, 1901),
and José Povill Ribera, *Rapsoda; Antología poetica para recitar* (Barcelona:
Occitanier, [1965] ).

# INDEX OF AUTHORS, COMPILERS, AND EDITORS

# INDEX OF TITLES

For works entered without author or compiler